GOD-MOMENTS IN THE AFRICAN JUNGLE

BY DR. PAUL R. KEIDEL

COPYRIGHT

First Printing: 2020 ISBN   978-1-67813-997-1

Content ID: 26320999

Published by PK3-Prints
1330 Upstream Farm Rd.
Forks, PA 18045

Visit us on Facebook at "Pkeidel Prints"

All Scripture quotations from the New International Version© 1984 edition of the Bible.

Cover photo of traditional art contributed by Ronald Brown.

ISBN 978-1-67813-997-1

9 781678 139971   90000

DEDICATED TO THE

Millions of Men and Women

Boys and Girls

In Africa

Who sacrifice daily to

fully follow Jesus

ENDORSEMENTS

I thank the Lord daily for these friends who read my stories and are willing to share their encouraging words with you.

"Paul Keidel revives the lost genre of missionary storytelling by recounting miracle after miracle of God's relentless pursuit of His lost ones in the remote African bush. Much credit goes to the author for his diligent chronicling of these remarkable events from his early childhood as a missionary kid in the Belgian Congo through his return to Africa as an adult, where he and his family served for 20 years. This is storytelling at its finest and will captivate readers—and entire families—with faith-filled adventures and divine wonders that brought many to the feet of Jesus."

Peter Burgo—Editor: *A-Life Magazine*
of the Christian & Missionary Alliance

"My boys Really enjoyed this, especially the second part! By the end of the book, they had been asking me not to forget to read to them! We were so blessed... Boys, especially, need exposure to the work of God through ministry work. Thank you!"

Katie Crowell, Home-schooling mother of nine

"Once called the "dark continent," Africa today has a growing brightness as the light of Jesus continues to bring salvation, hope and freedom from fear. Paul's stories are excellent examples of God at work in Africa. Having grown up in Africa like Paul and then worked alongside him during his decade in Congo, I can attest to the very significant work done by Paul due in part to his excellent understanding of African culture and his strong fluency in the local language."

Dr Ron Brown, Mission Coach
https://ronaldbrown.ca/global-vault/

"I stand amazed of the power of God as I read Move this Mountain! What a great book that will capture the heart of all readers, specifically children between the ages of 5-12 years. The well written adventures create excitement and a deeper understanding of what God is doing around the world. I would strongly recommend families to read this book together so they hear Matthew 28:19-20 come to life and ignite a passion within their family for missions."

Kris Smoll, Executive Director of Discovery Land Global,
Appleton Alliance Church Discovery Land, www.Dlglobal.org

"Paul Keidel's book illuminates the truth that God is reaching out in love to everyone, no matter where they are. His powerful stories of God's Kingdom being built here on earth demonstrate that miracles happen when we live out our calling to make disciples of all nations."

Dr. Erick Schenkel, former Executive Director of Jesus Film Project and author of *"Everyone, Everywhere"*

"We need to inspire children and youth with God's Word and with the lives of the saints. When we read about God's faithfulness and power in the lives of other believers, it gives us courage to step out in faith and to press on for His Kingdom. I pray that Paul's stories will be used mightily to stir the hearts of young men and women to faith and faithfulness."

Tom Chilton, Global Ministries, Awana®

"It is one thing to attend church for an hour each week. It is quite something else to be a living, breathing, walking Bible for people living in Africa in the Congo and Guinea for 20 years. For two decades, Paul Keidel faced suspicion, tribal witch doctors, black magic, armed rebels, malaria and harsh living conditions to bring the Good News of Jesus Christ to the people of these two nations. This is a book of miracles that transformed lives and brought Christianity to the hearts and minds of these good people. Paul Keidel is a missionary who follows the example of Paul the Apostle."

Biff Price – Author of the Stonebreaker Trilogy
https://www.sevenhornspublishing.com/the-reconstructionists

When God shows up unexpectedly in our day,

it's a "God-Moment" of His Love.

"...for His compassions never fail.
[23] They are new every morning;
Great is your faithfulness."
(Lamentations 3:22b-23)

INTRODUCTION

Did you ever wish your day would end without any hindrance or hang-up? You would say that life is a success because God gave you a straight and smooth road. But sometimes mountains loom high.

Mountains are challenges that seem way too steep to climb.

What do you do when you face mountains?

These stories describe day-to-day life in the African jungle when surprises happened that seemed like a mountain. These were moments when God intervened—"God-Moments"—and He helped people through.

Job, the biblical patriarch of suffering, thought he had his life in order. His road seemed smooth and straight. He had herds of camels and sheep, servants to care for his flocks, happy children, great wealth that set him apart from his friends, and wisdom that other people sought. He was a shining example of the blessings of the prosperity gospel. Life was great! His way was *"set"*. His life was positive and progressing wonderfully. People often feel like life makes sense when their way is *"set"* (with no mountains). It's a smooth path ahead.

Then disaster hits! A huge mountain! God permitted Satan, the enemy of our souls, to test Job's faith. Job quickly lost everything. His wealth and family (except his wife) were taken from him by natural disasters. Then he lost his health. Job's friends told him he was not wise—not even smart! When this happens today, our modern health-wealth-prosperity friends would point at us like Job's friends pointed at him and say, "God is punishing you 'cause you're hiding sin!"

Job wondered what God was doing to him. God had "upset" his success. Job thought, "Why should I, a good person, suffer? Why do I deserve this?" We often ask the same question when we are *"upset"*. Suddenly there is a mountain ahead and the road suddenly challenges us.

However, Job would not "accuse God." He didn't bail out on his faith, nor did he give up on God. In his faithfulness, he clung to the fact that his *"Redeemer still lives."* His thoughts were changing, but not his God.

In deep pain, he began to think differently about his relationship with the Almighty. That's when he developed a deeper knowledge of God that carried him through. God *"re-set"* Job's thoughts and beliefs and he found God's way through.

We often live the same experience. We have learned from the pain and have climbed beyond the obstacle. Now our road looks clear again, even though we may not understand all of the reasons for the *"upset."* And now we look differently at the smooth road.

God deliberately steps into our experience when we feel the same cycle of faith as Job, and He *"re-sets"* us. These are the three steps of a God-moment: (1) we feel oriented and *set* to the good life, (2) then bad things *upset* us and disorient life, (3) but then He steps in and *re-sets* us to the deeper things we learn through this moment with God.

This series of stories from Dr. Paul & Marian Keidel's African life tells you about true "mountains" that God overcame in "God-moments." These stories will lead you to a deeper understanding of the ways that God *re-sets* our good beliefs, and in the process, he *re-sets* our not-so-wonderful faith. As you read each story, identify those whom God *re-set*, and notice how each one responded.

Marian and Paul Keidel don't claim that their life with God is superior to anyone, but they do know Him as their always-present Friend. Just as they learned through these experiences, you may learn how God comes into our lives for His purposes because He loves us. And if we are called to His purpose, which is to *"be conformed to the image of Christ"* (Rom 8:28-32), we will let Him *re-set* us.

Allow these stories to show your "God-Moments" when you hear His Voice and discover His compassion.

CHAPTER 1
A DART TO HIS HEART

The Cessna single engine plane, loaded with baggage and two families, banked into landing position over the Congo River as it approached the Boma airport in the Democratic Republic of Congo (then called Zaire).

The pilot was aiming for a dirt airstrip next to the "terminal" building, a cement shed that looked like a two-car garage. The air traffic controller was yelling broken English phrases into his microphone, not knowing that the Mission Aviation Fellowship (MAF) pilot was going to land even though he couldn't understand the final approach instructions. There was no apparent danger of collision since this was probably the only flight of the week. But there was a slight danger of smashing goats that calmly ate lunch on the grassy landing strip.

Marian and Paul Keidel looked down from the descending plane at the red dirt strip of goats munching the runway. A man waving a big stick drove the goats away just before the plane touched down, blowing a cloud of dust.

The plane taxied through the dust to a grassy parking area by the terminal shed. A man appeared rolling a fire extinguisher up to the plane's engine. He was the fireman, ready to put out possible flames! Could one man do that? The passengers had no way of knowing if the canister contained enough chemical to douse a fire! The couple stared out the windows. Their familiar life in Michigan had come to this!

"Lord, what in the world did you get us into?" they wondered. Boma was a long way from home.

Paul had grown up in the Belgian Congo. His Mennonite parents were church planting missionaries among the BaShilele people. The BaShilele were headhunters. They lived in terror of the vengeance of demonic spirits. The village medicine man could command evil spirits to harass or kill anyone who stepped out of line. Diseases were physical proof of a nasty spirit in the body, and death was seen as the final attack of evil beings.

In the beginning of his parent's ministry a few of the native people liked what they heard about Jesus. When they submitted to the power of Christ, they were joyful that He took away their shame of sin and protected them from the demons. When they discovered peace with God, other family members came, followed by clan-groups, and finally, a whole tribe came to Jesus and was transformed by the Holy Spirit.

Paul trusted Jesus to change his heart as a little boy. However, from age six until sixteen, he lived in trauma. He had to change schools six times, and experienced two civil wars, one that required his family to escape from harm!

New teachers, new rules, new campuses, new classmates, new houses, new churches—it was finally too much! His heart was hiding, and he learned to ignore his emotions. Paul feared changes, and he built a hidden cocoon of safety within himself, while outwardly showing coolness to others.

He hid in his cocoon until age seventeen when he went off to a Christian college. Once there, he thought he saw many hypocrites all around him. They all claimed to be Christians, but some of them weren't *transformed*. This bothered him, "Why do they claim to be a Christian if they don't want to live it?" he wondered.

One day, the Holy Spirit shot a dart into his heart, "You call yourself a Christian?" He said, "You say you love Jesus with all of your heart, but you don't want Jesus to guide your decisions? Aren't you the biggest hypocrite?"

Wow! He'd never thought of that!

He took a long walk in a park to talk with Jesus. No one would hear this conversation.

"Lord Jesus," Paul prayed, "I am afraid of all the change that comes with life. Will You lead me so that I know each step You want me to take?"

"I will." Jesus responded.

Paul prayed, "If You can help me know each step, I'll go wherever You lead me."

Paul felt like Jesus was standing there right next to him. Jesus took his hand and said, "It's a deal!" The decision was firm.

Paul heard God speak that day. He came into Paul's life and changed him forever. From that moment, the Holy Spirit led Paul step by step—first to choose the direction in school studies. Then, God brought Paul and Marian together.

Marian had grown up in western Michigan in a Christian home. She was active in a local Baptist church where missionaries were a part of her childhood. She asked Jesus to forgive her and be her Lord when she was five years old. A few years later she knew God wanted her to be a missionary teacher.

She and Paul began their journey together. They went to see Holiday on Ice for their first date. For three years they learned more about each other and prayed for guidance. Together, they heard Jesus speak to them about serving Him as a family.

Now, back in Boma, they climbed out of the plane—thankfully they didn't need the fireman. A delegation of Congolese pastors and missionaries began to sing *Tonda Nzambi* [Thank you God]. There was a prayer, and then handshakes all around. They had arrived at their destination and new home.

Paul remembered hearing the words of God to the Prophet Jeremiah, *"Before I formed you in the womb I knew you, before you were born I set you apart"* (Jeremiah 1:5).

What was God planning for them?

THOUGHT QUESTIONS:
CHAPTER 1
A DART TO HIS HEART

Paul and Marian grew up in different homes and different families. Yet, God chose them and watched over them through their growing up years for His special purpose. These experiences came together in the events of this chapter.

1.   Read Jeremiah 1:1-9—How did God call Jeremiah? Memorize Jeremiah 1:5.

2.   How did the Holy Spirit use Paul's past experiences to reset his relationship with Jesus?

3.   What promise did the Holy Spirit make that gave Paul assurance?

4.   What promises from Jeremiah 1:1-9 give you assurance that God has chosen you?

CHAPTER 2
GOD'S WORDS—YOUR MOUTH

The Keidels made their home in Kinkonzi, a village in the Congo equatorial rain forest. Christian and Missionary Alliance (C&MA) missionaries had established Kinkonzi in the 1890s.

The sun rose at 6:00 a.m. and set at 6:00 p.m., but the forest grew so close to their house that they didn't see the sun until 8:00 a.m., and the evening shadows fell early at 4:00 p.m.

As they learned the Kikongo language, they began teaching at the Bible Institute.

Because the school had been founded in 1918, Paul was happy to discover that there were many good courses about teaching the Bible, preaching and Christian Education. However, there was nothing to help young men and women learn how to establish a community of believers in places without Christians. Further research revealed that in the Mayombe forest region, about half the size of Pennsylvania, there were almost 1000 villages without a Gospel witness.

Paul asked a student, "If you were sent to a place with no Christians what would you do? How would you begin?"

The student looked bewildered and shrugged his shoulders. "Kadi zaba." [No idea] he answered.

"Isn't that strange?" Paul thought. "They are learning how to be pastors and evangelists but they still don't know what to do!"

Paul decided to discuss the problem with Carol, another professor.

"Carol, how will they learn to start a church?" Paul asked her.

"That's just it, Paul. They guess! It's trial and error," she answered.

"What if I started a class about the art of church planting? Do you think the Director would like that?"

"That would be wonderful!" she exclaimed. "But, be ready for his response. He'll say they already learned this in the class on personal evangelism."

"What does that class teach?"

"They memorize Bible verses." Carol replied.

"Should I try to convince him anyway?" Paul inquired.

"Yes!" she encouraged him.

Paul walked home to think about how he would approach the Director with the idea. He asked Marian to pray about it with him, and they to put together a plan. He'd never taught the subject before, and he wanted the Holy Spirit's guidance before he went to see the Director.

When he felt he was ready, Paul knocked on the Director's office door.

"Yes, come in," he called out. Paul entered and sat down. He said a silent prayer, and began. "Mr. Director, I know that you've been here a long time, and you know the good and necessary things the students need to learn. I've been wondering what you might think about a class that teaches the graduates how to plant a church in villages where there are no Christians?"

"That's true, there is no class like that," the Director said, "but we teach them personal evangelism methods."

Paul continued, "What do they learn?"

"They learn how to share their faith, to talk about Jesus; and Bible verses." he replied.

Paul said, "It is really good that they learn Bible verses and how to share their faith, but what if a District Superintendent sends a student where there is not even one Christian? What does the student do?"

"Good question," the Director said.

"Let me describe my idea." Paul replied, smiling. "The course would be designed for just the senior class, and meet three times a week. We would use the Bible as the text to learn how the New Testament Apostles did it. On Saturdays, I would take them to a village where there are no Christians. We would continue going to that village until there were enough believers who could lead themselves."

18

"Oh, Mr. Paul…," the Director exclaimed, "that would be great! When should we start?"

Paul hadn't thought about that, so he said cautiously. "Well…we could start next semester, or in the next school term," he suggested.

The Director said, "Let's begin in January…and all seniors will take the class!" It was early December. Paul had just three weeks to prepare.

Paul walked across the campus wondering what had just happened. He hadn't expected such a positive response. His idea had produced a bigger answer than he had anticipated!

"It must be God's idea!" he mused.

But now, he had another problem. Not only had he never taught such a course before, but there was no known lesson guide in French or Kikongo. The lessons he would teach would influence many students. He remembered God's words to a prophet many years before, *"I have put my words in your mouth"* (Jeremiah 1:9).

"That's it! Let Him speak through me!" Paul concluded.

THOUGHT QUESTIONS:
CHAPTER 2
GOD'S WORDS—YOUR MOUTH

Sometimes we like to think that we have all of the answers, and so we don't depend on the Holy Spirit to guide us. But when we decide to listen and follow His voice, we begin to hear Him, even in surprising ways. Following His advice may lead us in a completely different direction than we planned, but it is always the best way.

1.   Read Acts 8:26-40: In what ways did God put His words into Philip's mouth? Memorize Jeremiah 1:9.

2.   What people did God use to lead Pastor Paul, and how did He use them to reset Paul's thinking?

3.   What new thoughts did God reset in Paul's mind?

4.   What might the Holy Spirit ask you to do that would require advice from more mature Christians?

CHAPTER 3
THE ANCESTORS TOLD US

Everyone wanted to take Paul's class, but only seniors were permitted. The nine men and two ladies were enthusiastic that they would learn how to plant a church in an un-evangelized village. They plunged into their New Testaments to see what the Apostles did. Finally, the week came for their first adventure in planting a new church.

It was Friday, and Paul was concentrating on Kikongo language study when two students came to the door.

"Koko [knock-knock], Pastor Paul."

"Come in, sit down!"

After they greeted each other the older of the two students began, "Have you asked permission from the village Chieftain where we will go tomorrow?"

Paul had been told that this was the protocol to follow, but no one had explained the proper procedure. "No, but we do need to do that! Would you go with me to ask permission?

The older student said, "Yes, let's go."

Paul had never planted a church in an un-evangelized village in Mayombe, but he had seen his father do so many times in the Kasai region. However, this was a different challenge. Here he was leading this class, and he didn't know how to do it the Yombe way. He would have to follow the Spirit's leading and watch his students. He had much to learn and improve upon.

The three men took the SUV over the rough, hole-filled jungle road. Their first stop was at the village of Kindi[1]. Some ladies came to the car. After the greetings, Paul asked in the Kikongo language, "Is the Chief here? We'd like to come tell your village about Jesus."

---

[1] All names of places and people in this collection of stories have been modified for their protection.

The women looked excited but perplexed. They answered, "That's wonderful, but the priest is doing it this week."

"Oh!" responded a student, "we'll come back another time!"

They drove down another muddy jungle road. After avoiding deep holes for a half hour, and covering about five miles, the older student suggested turning into the village of Kibu. They drove between two rows of huts for about 100 yards and stopped in front of the palaver hut. In Yombe villages the palaver hut usually sits in the village center and protects the Talking Drum[2]. The elders make important village decisions next to the drum.

As Pastor Paul and the students got out of the car a man came walking toward them from his house. He was the village Chief, and the timing was perfect!

Paul asked if they could talk with him and his elders.

The Chief gave an order, "Go to the Talking Drum and call the elders!"

They went to the palaver hut, sat down and talked while the drummer beat out the message.

> *"The white man has come.*
> *The white man has come.*
> *Gather and talk."*

After fifteen minutes four older men came out of the forest from their fields. They placed their machetes on the ground and sat down. They looked at Paul, waiting for him to speak. What should he do? He'd never done this before!

Paul took a deep breath to ease his nervousness, and began speaking to them through a translator to make sure that he didn't make any language mistakes.

---

[2] Their tradition states that the Talking Drum's life never ends, but goes to sleep. This is because its ability to communicate gives it a life of its own.

(Later, his fluency in the Kikongo language would be much better and he would no longer need the help of an interpreter).

"We are from Kinkonzi Bible School where these men are learning how to tell people about Jesus." Paul pointed to the students. "We would like to come to your village to talk about the Jesus Way, because it is by walking in that Way that people come to God. Would we be able to tell your people about the Jesus Way?" he asked them.

The first elder acted in the role of mediator for the Chief, and he repeated the whole message to the Chief, as if he hadn't heard anything.

The Chief responded with a lengthy explanation that meant, "No."

Paul, thinking that his explanation wasn't clear, made his request again in a different way, "We aren't here to fight over religion and arguments. My students only want to speak to your people about the Voice of God that came to us from Jesus. Would you permit us to tell your people about the Voice of God?"

The Chief spoke up stopping the elder, "The ancestors told us that one day someone will come with the Voice of God. When he comes, we must receive him. If we refuse, we will be in big trouble with God! When will you come?"

Paul didn't realize just what had happened in that moment, but the translator had used the local words *"mbembo aNzambi"* [Voice of God]. God had planted this word in the village heart centuries before. They knew that someday someone would come. Paul discovered that when that phrase was used, their hearts opened like magic because the Voice of God had finally arrived. When this was explained, Paul was both stunned and happy!

"May we come tomorrow night?" Paul asked, not wanting to wait until a later time.

"Come tomorrow night at sunset. My people will be ready," promised the Chief.

Paul left the meeting amazed at what had happened. He hadn't expected to meet people whose ears were so ready to hear the Gospel!

23

"What is happening?" he wondered.

God had placed a key phrase, the Voice of God, in the Chieftain's heart. It is exactly what the Apostle Paul describes, *"since what may be known about God is plain to them, because God has made it plain to them"* (Romans 1:19).

The Voice of God had come to Kibu! Now, the challenge was to work with the Spirit who would reset these people's hearts!

THOUGHT QUESTIONS:
CHAPTER
THE ANCESTORS TOLD US

God has placed within the heart of every culture an understanding of Himself. People may not know the Bible or all of the words of Jesus, but they know deep down inside that there is a Supreme God who wants a relationship with them. However, most of them do not know how to find God until someone comes with the Story of Jesus. And that deep -down-inside awareness comes alive when they hear the Story.

We learned in this story how God prepared the village Chieftain for the coming of the Gospel. Paul was both blessed and surprised to learn how they had been waiting.

1.   Read Psalm 19:1-6 and Romans 1:18-23. Memorize Psalm 19:1-2.

2.   In what ways do these verses state that God makes His presence known to people?

3.   What did God place in the villager's heart that made them ready?

4.   What are some things around you that already show that God is there waiting for you?

CHAPTER 4
MOVE THIS MOUNTAIN!

They were deep in the jungle and didn't know what to do! The students were standing knee deep in red mud. They wondered why the good things that just happened in Kibu should end this way!

Their first visit to Kibu began so well.

Eleven students—nine men and two women—rode through the jungle so they could keep their promise to the Chieftain. They were anxious about two things. First, the Chieftain said that his village had waited many years to hear the Voice of God. Now the students wanted to be sure that his people heard the Good News of Jesus.

Second, they were anxious because the clouds over the jungle were looming very dark and menacing. Would their meeting be washed out? They prayed that it would not be cancelled.

They bounced their way over the soggy jungle path. The 4 x 4-SUV pulled them through mud bogs as deep as the wheels. The thunder rolled in the sky and six miles seemed like one hundred.

Suddenly, the vehicle came into a jungle opening. They drove down the center street between the huts. The passengers piled out in front of the palaver roof that protected the Talking Drum, the same roof where Paul had met the Chief yesterday.

Children came running from everywhere. Some seemed to pop out of the jungle and into the village clearing. They rarely saw a car in their village— this must mean something special was coming tonight.

The students immediately formed into their teams of two each and began visiting the homes.

Making their way across the village, they talked with people about knowing God. Their goal was to visit every family and pray for them—every need was brought to Jesus.

The skies kept grumbling and the clouds got angry. Some people anxiously looked up wondering what would happen.

Mwanda and his teammate stopped to greet a woman who looked uncomfortable. She was sitting on a stool alone in front of her hut. Her legs were so bloated that she could not move them. She was suffering from a debilitating tropical disease of elephantiasis. A microscopic parasite, called a Filarial worm, enters the blood stream by a bug bite. It multiplies making many invisible worms that plug the lymph glands. This hinders blood flow so legs and limbs lack the needed blood flow and supply. As a result, limbs bloat.

The students greeted her and asked how they could pray for her. She told them how she suffered so much pain and could not work or take care of little ones. And now she depended on others to live. "I want peace in my soul," she begged.

Mwanda responded. "We are so sorry for your suffering. We are here to tell you the Good News that Jesus suffered just like we do and for that reason we are told, 'come before Him with courage and pray…'"

She shook her head, "Yes, that must be true."

The student continued, "Jesus died on the cross to give us that peace. Mama, do you believe that Jesus can forgive you?"

"Inga Tata," [yes Mister] she responded, as she raised a hand.

"Then please pray with me and you will ask Jesus to forgive you."

Everyone bowed their heads and she repeated after him, "Jesus, I know that you died on the cross for my sins … I know that you are the only Son of God who can forgive … forgive me because I am a sinner."

After she repeated the simple words, he continued praying, "Jesus: Mama suffers much pain and loneliness. She can't even walk right. Would you bring honor to your Name when you touch her legs and body and give healing to her body just like you did to her soul? Ameni."

She thanked them profusely and asked if soon in the future they could baptize her. She had heard somewhere that people need to be baptized as a testimony of belonging to the Jesus Tribe. The students promised to ask the pastor.

The clouds rumbled even more!

As people came to the Chieftain's house, rain-drops began to fall. He called out to everyone, "Come into my house quickly." Nearly forty people plus children squeezed into his large front room.

As the rain pounded on the tin roof, the students taught them a new song about Hope in the Name of Jesus. One student taught about how that One Name is our only hope for forgiveness and peace with God. As the rain subsided, the students invited anyone who wanted this Peace to talk with them.

That night only three people prayed to receive the Peace of Jesus—the Chieftain, a village elder, and the lady.

Paul wondered why there was such a small response, but remembered that we speak the Gospel and the Holy Spirit brings the response. Little did he know that one week from today they would see how deep the truth had gripped the Chieftain's soul.

The students climbed in the SUV to ride home. Eleven people in a vehicle that holds six was tight. They were quiet. They wondered how the storm had changed the road that now looked like a moving stream.

As they drove on the pitch-dark jungle trail, the lights only showed a track on the moving water-way. Paul tried to discern where to guide the wheels. When they came to the first mud bog, he only saw water and muck. He couldn't guess where to go except through the middle.

Suddenly the vehicle lurched, fell and stopped. Paul looked out the window; all four tires were spinning like they were in the air. The 4 x 4 was hi-centered by the deep bog because the frame sat on hard dirt, but the wheels were spinning in water. He looked around at all the dark trees. If they had a winch, they could tie the cable to one and pull themselves out. Unfortunately, Paul had borrowed a car without a winch. There was no help in this jungle bog.

"Everyone out! We are stuck!" Paul called out.

Shoes came off, pant legs and skirts were adjusted up and everyone stepped into the knee-deep muck. The night was very dark. They could hear the jungle animals calling in the trees. The students were sure they would spend the whole night here—or maybe longer. Eleven people can't move a two-ton truck when it is stuck without traction.

That's when someone said, "We better pray!"

Paul pointed to Baza who was nearest, "You pray!"

Paul didn't know how to pray this time. He even wondered if it mattered. It all seemed like an impossible mountain!

Knee deep in gooey red mud gave new meaning to the words "bogged down!" And prayer was all they knew!

Everyone put their hand on the vehicle. Baza looked up to the dark forest canopy and began to pray, "Dear Jesus, You said that a little faith can move mountains. Now we have a mountain that has to be moved. This car that is made with human hands, is stuck! It is really stuck in the muck. Move this mountain in Jesus' Name! Ameni"

Everyone agreed, "Ameni!"

They looked at the wheels and saw how deeply the truck was in the muck. Some wondered if they could find the bog bottom. One student stepped back into the grassy ditch and stumbled on some logs. Everyone turned to help him but recognized that he had fallen onto God's answer.

They began to scheme as a team. They chose a log to put under each tire to give a bottom to the bog. Then they took a longer log and made it into a lever to lift one side of the vehicle.

A leader instructed the young ladies, "Now, three of us will pull down on this lever that is above our heads. As we pull down, the other end will raise up the truck. Other guys will lift the truck with their own hands. When you ladies see the wheels come out of the water, push the logs into the rut under the tires so that the car comes down resting on the logs. This way we will make a bridge."

Everyone got in place.

They counted, "One! Two! Three! LL-III-FF-TT!"

The two tons of steel lifted out of the muck and the tires slurped free. Quickly the ladies slid the logs in the bog and the wheel weight came down on the new bridge. It worked! The car did not sink down.

They repeated the same action on the other side so that the vehicle sat on its own bridge on logs above the bog.

Then Paul climbed into the driver's seat. He shifted into low four-wheel drive. Each person found a position to push.

"Ready?" Paul asked above the roar of the motor.

As he engaged the clutch the tires grabbed the logs and two tons of steel jumped forward riding on the mire. They were free!

Everyone piled in the car with mud on their clothes. But they sang all the way home praising Jesus that He had moved the mountain.

Just like Jesus promised, *"… If anyone says to this mountain, 'Go, throw yourself into the sea,' and does not doubt in his heart but believes that what he says will happen, it will be done for him* (Mark 11:23)."

Paul's faith grew a bit deeper as he realized that when it is God's work, we work together with Him.

But next week would bring a bigger surprise!

THOUGHT QUESTIONS:
CHAPTER 4
MOVE THIS MOUNTAIN!

Often life experiences become challenges that we feel like we can't overcome. The way we look at them will determine how God can intervene. Our perspective of God and daily life largely determine how He is able to help us.

1.   Mark 11:20-24—Why is it important to believe and not doubt? Memorize Mark 11:23.

2.   What different challenges did the students pray for in this story? What was God's answer to those prayers?

3.   List three "mountains" that challenge you and begin praying for Him to answer.

CHAPTER 5
EYES WIDE OPEN

At their last visit, Paul saw how the people in the village of Kibu wanted the Voice of God. The bigger surprise was that the Chief wanted Paul's students to come and talk about Jesus right away. However, God saved an eye-opening surprise for their second night.

Chief Raymond made sure that the entire village was present. One hundred and thirty people sat on the ground in his court-yard waiting for songs to begin. The Chief and his elders sat along the left side of the open area, and families filled the remaining space, while the smaller children squatted on the front row.

A Coleman lantern lit the square, and the darkness of the jungle evening created a black circular wall around the assembly.

The first student gave a beautiful sermon about the crucifixion and resurrection of Jesus, telling them that this event was the one sacrifice that God accepts that will forgive their sins.

A second student invited them to choose the Jesus Way. "You heard God's Voice tonight that Jesus's death and resurrection are all we need to trust if we want Him to forgive us of our sins. Tonight, there may be some who want to talk about this. Perhaps you have questions? We invite you to stay seated where you are. We know some of you want to get back to your meal preparation, and you may leave now. We are happy to talk with anyone who stays behind."

The crowd was silent and nobody moved. The student didn't know what to do! Did they understand?

He turned and whispered to Pastor Paul, "What do I do?"

"Explain it again; maybe they didn't understand." Paul instructed.

The student explained it again, but they sat silently—even the babies stopped crying.

He turned in panic to his professor who was supposed to know. "Now what?" His eyes were wide open and worried.

Paul said, "Perhaps they have something to say to you. Ask them."

The student turned to them, "Is there something you'd like to tell us?"

The head elder spoke for the Chief, "You said if we want God to forgive us, that we should stay seated. Everyone wants God to forgive them—so we sit."

The student again turned to Paul his eyes wide open in amazement. This was not expected. "What do we do now?"

Paul said, "Divide them into groups, and each student will lead them to trust Christ." They had learned the verses to lead others to Jesus; now it was time to use them!

That night the whole village came to Christ in one decision!

When Paul returned home that night, overwhelmed by what had happened, he spoke to the Lord. "God, I thought a miracle like this only happens in other peoples' stories, but now You have made it happen here!"

God had taught Paul a lesson in Kibu: "I want You follow My plan, not your plan!"

Like the prophet Isaiah said, *"See, the former things have taken place, and new things I declare; before they spring into being, I announce them to you"* (Isaiah 42:9).

God sometimes appears in our personal story when we least expect Him.

THOUGHT QUESTIONS:
CHAPTER 5
EYES WIDE OPEN

God will sometimes surprise us so He can teach us a new lesson. He does this when He knows that certain ideas that we believe are not His ideas. That's when He comes to us with a big surprise to our plans that forces us to think again and "reset" our ideas. In this story, God's Spirit opened everyone's mind to a new thing.

1. Read Isaiah 42:9, Acts 10:1-48—How did the Holy Spirit open Peter's eyes to the new truth from God in Acts 10?

2. How did this upset Peter's thoughts and reset them? Memorize Isaiah 42:9—what does God promise to do to certain thoughts we think?

3. What lessons did God teach Paul and the students that reset their ideas about deciding to follow Jesus? Why was this a surprise?

4. What if you planned for something to happen a certain way, but suddenly the Holy Spirit changed things—how would you correctly respond to His reset?

CHAPTER 6
OPPOSITION SOFTENED

When Christ-followers take the Gospel into the Enemy's territory, he will fight back! The Bible teaches that Satan is the Enemy of our souls, and he is like a lion sneaking around looking for anyone he can devour (1 Peter 5:8). That means he will oppose you and make trouble!

Two years passed before a new group of students was able to begin in the village of Kindi. The Chief was very happy that someone would bring them the Voice of God, and the meetings began.

During the first month, Paul and his students encountered a man named Tamo. He said, "I'm a Christian and my name is Tamo. I will help you."

However, Pastor Paul felt that something about Tamo was not right, and he wondered what the man really wanted.

His students were also very suspicious of the man's intentions. Tamo was persistent, and he walked through the village with them watching everything they did. When Pastor Paul was in Kindi, Tamo never left him alone. The villagers seemed hesitant and fearful when Tamo was watching. He was deceitful and sly.

By October, the students were worried. They told Pastor Paul that Tamo was hindering them. They said, "People aren't responding because of what Tamo does when we are absent!"

Pastor Paul wrote to pastors in the USA asking them and their congregations to pray that this man would stop hindering the Gospel.

Early in December the mail carrier stopped at Pastor Paul's house.

"Koko Koko" he called, "*nkanda kwa Pasteur Paul.*" [A letter to Pastor Paul].

Paul thanked him for the letter. It was from a church in Olympia, Washington, USA. The pastor described that he was burdened for Paul and Marian's ministry. He had asked his congregation to pray two times a week that the Holy Spirit would change Tamo's heart by March 30th, a date that was four months from the time that the letter had been written.

Paul took the letter to the students. As he read it, they excitedly proclaimed that they, too, must pray that something would happen by March 30th. So, every class period from December forward, the students and the Christians in Olympia were praying that Tamo's heart would change.

Would Tamo hear God's Voice?

One Saturday evening in February, at the end of a prayer and worship meeting in Kindi, the speaker asked the villagers if anyone wanted to receive forgiveness from Jesus. No one in the crowd of 150 responded. Nobody moved—absolute silence!

Suddenly, a little nine-year old boy began to whimper and then cry. His friends scolded him, "Be quiet! Don't embarrass us!"

Lufua, the lead student evangelist, went to the boy. "Stand up little one," he ordered. "What do you want?"

The boy stayed sitting on the ground whimpering.

"Stand up little one, tell us what you want!" he repeated.

He was about to scold the boy when the child said, "I can't stand up. My legs don't work. I want Jesus to fix my legs just like in your story," he cried.

The crowd moved away a few steps. Lufua looked at Pastor Paul asking what to do.

"Call his mother," Paul said.

She came out of the crowd and Lufua asked, "Is he your boy?"

"Yes, Evangelist." she answered.

"Will you allow us to pray for him?" Lufua asked.

"Yes, you may." she responded.

Someone picked him up and placed him in the middle of the crowd with his mother. Lufua wanted everyone to see. The students crowded around the boy and began to pray as the villagers pushed closer to hear. All were quiet.

"Jesus, please show your glory. Heal him by your powerful Name," pleaded one.

"Holy Spirit come on him and in the Name of Jesus, heal him," asked another.

The crowd looked on, wondering, "What kind of God is this?"

When the prayer ended, Lufua asked the mother to pick him up. He crawled on her back and left as the students encouraged her to trust Jesus.

The vehicle was full of seven students going home that night, but they were very quiet. They, too, wondered how God might act.

The following Wednesday, Paul and Lufua were traveling through the village and were stopped by some women who wanted to travel with them to the market. Paul noticed some children playing soccer. Then he saw the boy—he was running and chasing the ball!

"Lufua!" exclaimed Paul, and pointed "Is that the little boy?"

Lufua looked, "Yes, it is!"

The boy was running with his friends!

The prophet Jeremiah said, *"Call to me and I will answer you and tell you great and unsearchable things you do not know"* (Jeremiah 33:3).

God had come to this boy.

The Holy Spirit was softening the hearts of the people.

Satan, the prowling lion, was losing influence.

THOUGHT QUESTIONS:
CHAPTER 6
OPPOSITION SOFTENED

Everybody likes a miracle. The Bible teaches that God will do a miracle to get our attention so He can teach us about Jesus. This story told us how God softened the people's hearts so they would want to hear more about the powerful Name of Jesus.

1.   Read Acts 3:1-11: How did God soften resistance to the Gospel? Memorize Jeremiah 33:3.

2.   What did God do to the villagers to soften their hearts and reset their thinking about Jesus?

3.   Why is prayer important to soften hearts?

4.   Ask a new Christian you know to tell you how God softened their heart so that they wanted to know more about Jesus.

CHAPTER 7:
DON'T PLAY WITH SATAN!

The opposition grew stronger!

On March 30th, there was a funeral at Kindi, but no one participated. Only Tamo buried the stranger. This was very unusual since, in this tribe, death is the biggest community event.

Why was Tamo required to bury the man alone and pay all the expenses? Why did the stranger die? Why would no one attend the event or even show sympathy?

Two months later in May, Pastor Paul was returning from another village at night and stopped in Kindi to pick up more students. Suddenly, Tamo appeared out of the night darkness to the driver's door. He wanted to talk to Paul. Not knowing what this would bring, Pastor Paul stepped out and moved into the brightness of the headlights so everyone would see and hear. Pastor Paul would not speak in secret with this evil man!

The students remained stuffed in the back of the vehicle. They strained their ears to hear what was being said. The village people came and formed a big circle around them to hear every word. Their curiosity surrounded Pastor Paul and Tamo in the middle

Tamo began pleading, "Pastor Paul, you must pray for me that Jesus will protect me from my enemies."

"Why?" asked Pastor Paul. "Who are they? What are they doing?"

Tamo described how, beginning on March 30th, everything was going wrong in his life. Now he feared someone had put a curse on him to kill him and his family.

Pastor Paul responded, "I would be happy to pray for you. However, Jesus only protects those who are in His family."

Tamo was indignant, "You mean I'm not in Jesus' family?"

"You know the answer in your heart," answered Paul. "All I can do is pray for your soul that it will get right with God. If you want me to pray for that, I'll be happy to pray."

Tamo was trapped in his words. The crowd was listening. If he refused, he would be shamed in front of them. He agreed, and Pastor Paul prayed that he would hear the Voice of God. Paul thought this would be their last meeting.

A short time later Tamo went to see the Bible School Director to ask that he mediate a conflict. He said to the Director, "I don't know why, but ever since Pastor Paul and the students have come to my village everything has gone wrong for me. Pastor Paul's power is greater than mine!"

The Director laughed. He knew that the Name of Jesus was gaining power. So, he refused to help Tamo.

Later, during a teacher's meeting, however, the Director did tell Paul about the conversation. Everyone laughed because they knew what was happening. The power of the Holy Spirit with the prayer of the faithful was acting in Tamo's life. God was working!

Tamo was the witch doctor who controlled the souls of his village. However, once the students and the Olympia Church began praying, the Power of Jesus slowly crumbled Tamo's evil kingdom. The students later learned that on March 30th Tamo had poisoned the head witch doctor. Tamo knew that killing the other evil man was playing with Satan. But he envied more of Satan's power. This was Tamo's mistake and now his actions came back to bite him.

Six months after the conversation in the headlights, Tamo, the witch doctor, prayed to trust Jesus as Savior. The students had learned to stand firm, to resist Satan, and to *"put on the whole armor of God"* (Ephesians 6:11).

THOUGHT QUESTIONS:
CHAPTER 7
DON'T PLAY WITH SATAN!

It is very dangerous to play with fire! Did your mom or dad ever tell you, "Be careful! Don't get burned!" This story told us about the danger of playing with Satan and his demons, which is more dangerous than playing with fire! Tamo wanted more of Satan's power. However, those evil powers could not resist against the Name of Jesus.

1.   Acts 18:13-20—in what ways does the Holy Spirit overcome the power of Satan? Memorize Ephesians 6:11.

2.   What did the students and the church in Olympia, WA (USA) do to weaken the power of Satan?

3.   How did the Holy Spirit upset Tamo's thinking?

4.   What will you do to be strong against Satan?

CHAPTER 8
GHOSTS—OUT YOU GO!

"Pastor Paul…," Mongo called, "…come quickly!"

Mongo was a strong evangelist and he learned quickly. But tonight, he looked worried. Obviously, he faced a problem he hadn't learned about.

"What is the problem?" Paul asked, as they walked to the end of the village.

"The man said that since two children died of measles one year ago no one has been able to sleep through the night," Mongo explained.

"Do you mean the sadness of the memory keeps them awake?" Paul inquired.

"No," answered Mongo, "It is more frightening than that."

They quickly arrived in front of a family's hut. The father, mother and two young children were sitting outside on low stools in a circle. Another student sat quietly waiting for them. They all looked frightened and confused.

"Mbot'eno." Paul greeted them and everyone shook hands. Someone brought two stools for Paul and Mongo, and they joined the circle.

"Abwe?" [What is the problem?] Paul asked.

The father began, "Last year our two babies died from measles. Since then, we have not been able to sleep!" he explained with a trembling voice.

"I'm sorry that your children are gone." Paul sympathized. "But, why is it that you cannot sleep?" Paul wondered why something that had happened the year before would keep them awake.

"Their spirits keep returning at night!" Father continued. "We can all go to sleep. But in the middle of the night one of the little ones will wake in a cold sweat feeling someone in the room. When she opens her eyes, she sees one of the dead children looming over her. She panics because she thinks the spirit has come to take her life, so she screams and we all wake up in a terror; and we are afraid for the rest of the night."

"How often does this happen?" Paul asked, knowing that what Americans and Europeans call ghosts are evil spirits in this part of Africa.

"It happens almost every night so that we are afraid to go to sleep. When we do fall into sleep a spirit comes to visit and we are afraid again!"

"I understand why you told the evangelists about this, but what can they do?" Pastor Paul asked.

"Your students keep telling us that your Jesus can do anything. They say that He is more powerful than anyone."

"Yes," Paul affirmed. "This is true. What would you like Jesus to do?"

"I want Him to stop the spirits from scaring us. I want Him to give us peace at night!" The father had heard God's Voice, and he hoped that Jesus could help.

Pastor Paul knew now that the father was ready to do anything to have peace. But the steps to freedom from evil spirits were costly to these people.

Paul said, "Jesus only protects people who are in His family. Jesus taught that we must love God and serve only Him. If you want Him to protect your family, then you must renounce anything or anyone that you have trusted to protect your family. You must trust only Jesus. Do you have any charms, amulets or images that you have purchased to protect you?"

Pastor Paul was learning the names of the local gods. People in this culture live in daily fear of a curse from an enemy. In order to protect themselves from vengeful curses, they pay the shaman [witchdoctor] [3] to make protective charms that they wear. For example, they tie a charm around a newborn's waist to protect him from a jealous woman who can't have her own child. They do not name the baby for one year after birth so that no one can invoke a death curse on the infant that has no identity.

---

[3] Shaman, witchdoctor, medicine man, sorcerer, etc. are all terms that describe the person who uses demon powers to protect people or to take vengeance on an enemy. He influences the evil spirits and demons through sacrifices, incantations, communicating with the dead, and other black magic methods.

The father hesitated, knowing that he now had to expose secrets of the magic arts. This could endanger his safety if the witchdoctor became angry with him for rejecting the power of the ancestral gods.

The father finally said, "No we don't have anything."

Mongo, who knew the culture well, also knew that the father lied. "How about the fetish of the evil eye? Or the fetish of the hair? Or the idol of the ancestors?" He named several types knowing that he would find one.

The father sighed, "Yes, we have all of those and more. We spent much money so that the fetishes would protect us from the curse of death."

"How many of them have worked so far?" Mongo asked.

"Kadi kiasa!" [nothing!] he exclaimed, as he smacked his hands together.

Paul continued, "You know where they are. Go! Get all of them and remove the ones you wear on your bodies! Bring them here. Jesus cannot protect you if you want another power to protect you."

The family went into the hut. Five minutes later they came out with a brown sack full of things.

"Dump them out, please," Paul asked.

The father opened the sack and dropped them on the ground.

"Now…" Paul spoke on a hunch, "…what's under your bed?"

Mongo said, "Go get it! You haven't brought everything."

The father jumped up and ran into the house. He came out with a statue. It was a gross representation of a person with a large head and torso, and small legs. He put it on the pile.

"What's that?" Pastor Paul asked.

"It's the god who protects us when we sleep," he answered.

"Did he protect your sleep?" Paul asked.

47

"No!" the family answered with one voice.

Mongo pressed further, "What else did you forget to bring out?"

Both parents affirmed, "That is all. We promise."

Then Paul began to instruct. "We must do like the Apostles did in the times of Jesus. We must burn all magic things of the Evil one, just like the Apostles. After they burned their magic things, Jesus was able to protect them. Will you burn these things?"

This was a frightening question. They had confessed to paying a high price for this protection. Now, to burn these things meant that they were rejecting the shaman. This could enrage him, and cause him to put new curses on them. Yet, Jesus taught that we must repent of our sins and renounce all other gods, and follow Him.

After much thought the father and mother said they wanted to burn everything, and turn away from the evil spirits. They took the kerosene lantern and, together, they went around back. The fetishes and idols were put in a pile and the lamp's kerosene was poured on the stack. They lit a flame to the fuel and watched the fire grill their gods while they sang:

> *"There is power, power, wonder working power,*
> *In the Blood, of the Lamb,*
> *There is power, power, wonder working power,*
> *In the precious blood of the Lamb."*

When all was burned and only ashes remained, they came back to their stools and sat together.

Pastor Paul continued, "You have done something that is very hard. You have declared that you are done with the power of the Evil One. Jesus teaches us that to follow Him, we must pray and ask Him to forgive our sins. He said to those who believe in the Son of God that He gives power to become His children. Will you do that now?"

"Yes, Tata," they said. "We want to follow Jesus."

Together, the family prayed asking Jesus to receive them into His family. There was joy all around, and Pastor Paul took them one more step closer to peace. "When you are in the Jesus clan, you can ask Him to protect you, to give you peace, and to keep away the evil spirits. You belong to God and God is your Father. This all happens because Jesus died and rose to show His power."

"Yes, Tata," the father said. "Now I know inside of me that He is there. I'm at peace."

"That is the Spirit of Jesus talking to your spirit," Paul affirmed. "Now let's go inside and pray for your house."

They entered the hut together. Everyone knelt on the dirt floor as each person began to pray that the Power Who destroyed the fetish curse, the Powerful Name of Jesus, would cleanse this house of every evil being.

The father prayed his first prayer with his family, "Jesus, come into this house and make it Your house. In Your name chase away all the evil beings that have been living here. It's Jesus' house!" he declared.

Another student evangelist prayed, "In the Name of Jesus, clean this house. Evil spirits," he called out to them, "by the Power of Jesus, leave this place! It is not your house anymore! Get out!"

As they prayed there was the sensation of movement out of the room, upward to the roof peak, and away. Then there was a calm.

Everyone finished praying. Pastor Paul pressed the truth of loyalty to Jesus. "Your house is clean. You are children of God. Jesus is your Savior and Protector. Don't go back to the shaman. Don't fear him, either. Neither he nor any of his curses can touch you."

Mongo added, "Don't ever pay for fetishes or idols again or you will open the door for the evil spirits to come back. Do you understand what has happened?"

"Yes, Tata," he said, "we will only follow Jesus."

A week later the team returned to Kibu. As they entered the village, Paul instructed Mongo and his partner, "First, go to that family. Ask them only one question, 'How did you sleep?'"

"Yes, Tata." The students left for the hut at the end of the row.

They found the father and mother preparing the evening meal. After the greeting, Mongo asked them, "How did you sleep this week?"

Both parents looked up with big smiles, "We never slept so good in a year! Everyone slept every night!"

God had come powerfully into their home. They knew the truth: *"You, dear children, are from God and have overcome them, because the One who is in you is greater than the one who is in the world"* (1 John 4:4).

THOUGHT QUESTIONS:
CHAPTER 8
GHOSTS—OUT YOU GO!

The Bible teaches that there are angels that come from God and will only obey Him. God's angels are messengers that He sends to His people to guide and bring people back to Him.

But Satan was an angel who rebelled against God and was removed from God's presence. Since that time, Satan, and his angels that fell with him, have harassed and troubled people. Jesus said that Satan's angels are our enemy and that they are like a thief who *"...comes to steal, and kill, and destroy"* (John 10:10). However, Jesus comes to give "abundant life" (John 10:10).

This story described ghosts. Remember that what we call ghosts may be evil angels. Never forget that the Holy Spirit who is in us is stronger than all evil spirits.

1.   Read Acts 16:16-40—How did evil spirits harass different people? Memorize 1 John 4:4.

2.   How did Satan make this village family become his slaves?

3.   Describe the steps the family took to get free. Who took the place of the "ghosts" in their house?

4.   What things must you avoid to stay free from the slavery of Satan and his demons?

CHAPTER 9
FREAK ACCIDENT—A GOD MOMENT

Pastor Paul and his student, Mongo, did not know that on this particular Thursday they would encounter danger. But someone in America was praying for them, and that the prayer was powerful.

They were traveling ten miles deep into the jungle, beyond Kibu, to the village of Kami.

On their way, they passed over a bridge made of logs and boards. They saw that the boards were loose. A crew of men were working on the bridge.

"I don't like the look of that." Paul said as they crossed over the bridge. Several weeks previously they had been traveling to another village for weekend meetings. As they had passed over a shaky log bridge the planks separated and the front tire fell through. He didn't want that to happen again!

Mongo was looking at the children playing in the water and at the work crew. "They're repairing something. I hope they finish before we come back. Otherwise, we may not be able to get back home."

They arrived safely at Kami and taught their class. After a quick meal, they got into the 4 x 4 to return home. A church Elder was returning to Kinkonzi with them. Paul had gladly invited him to come with them, not knowing he would be important to their survival.

As they slowly made their way down the jungle road, they rounded a curve and encountered a ten-year-old boy stripping bamboo into thin slats. As he cleaned the slats, he threw the unneeded scraps on the road. When he saw the approaching vehicle, he moved to the side of the road.

They waved to each other as they passed by.

Then it happened!

Paul heard a clicking noise underneath. Looking in the rear-view mirror he saw that a bamboo slat was snarled by the back bumper. The SUV's momentum whipped the opposite end of the slat towards the boy, and it struck him, slicing his knee like a sharp knife, and knocking him to the ground. He screamed as he fell!

Paul stomped on the brakes, ignoring the warning of the experienced Congolese pastors. They had warned him about the tradition in the Congo: Any auto driver who killed or injured someone would be severely beaten, if not killed. The cultural belief was that the driver was trying to kill the victim and take his soul to the land of the ancestors. As a result, the family of the victim must take vengeance and kill the driver.

"What happened?" asked Mongo.

"He's hurt...!" Paul yelled, as he opened the door and ran to the boy lying on the ground, holding his knee. He was crying and in great pain as blood streamed from his leg.

Mongo and the elder followed close behind. Paul tried to calm the boy as he examined his bleeding leg. The bamboo slat had sliced open his leg behind his knee. The wound was so deep that Paul saw the tendons.

"Thank you, Jesus!" prayed Paul, "It didn't cut an artery. We must help him!"

He ran to the car for the First Aid kit while Mongo and the Elder held the screaming boy. Paul returned with the kit, saying, "We need water for the boy to drink, and to wash the wound!"

"How can we give it to him?" asked the Elder. "We don't have any water or a cup!"

Mongo looked at the Elder's hat. "We'll use your hat! There's water in the stream!" He grabbed the man's hat off his head and ran to the creek under the bridge.

Paul took two aspirin from the kit. With the elder's hat full of water, he instructed the boy to drink. "Take this medicine. You will feel better."

Paul was hoping the aspirin would dull his pain, or that the boy might become calmer because Paul had comforted him!

"Let's put him in the car," Paul ordered. "But there can't be any blood on him. We need to find his mother in the village and take them to the hospital."

Mongo and the elder looked at Paul with fear in their eyes. They knew the dangerous tradition if the people decided to take vengeance.

They put the boy in the car and drove to the next village. The boy suddenly stopped crying. He had never ridden in a car before, and he had never taken aspirin. This was a new experience and it was fun! His eyes were big as he looked through the window at the trees going by.

They came to the village; Mongo and the Elder stepped into the fast-growing crowd, and Paul stayed in the car with the boy, hoping they would be safe.

"Who is the mother of this child?" asked the Elder. "Where is she?"

A teenager looked inside and saw the boy with a white bandage on his leg, but didn't see blood. "What happened?" he asked. Then he murmured with fear, "His father is our village Chieftain."

Paul was now even more worried because he had injured the Chieftain's son.

"Go quickly!" ordered the Elder. "Tell his mother to come, and that God has been with their son today."

Within seconds there was a large crowd standing around and gazing at the boy inside.

The boy was feeling more like a hero, and less like a victim! This was an exciting way to get attention.

The parents came. When the Elder smelled their breath, he knew they had been drinking palm wine. They were a bit shaky. The mother looked in the car and began to cry, "What happened to my boy?"

The Elder began, "Mama. Today God was with your child. He was hurt and it was a good thing that this white man was driving. He stopped and helped your son. He wants to take him to the doctor at Kinkonzi."

The father began to speak and gesture wildly, "What kind of trouble is this? My boy was working! How was he hurt?"

Mongo tried to calm the half-drunk man, "Tata Chief. Today God was with your child. He was hurt. His leg was cut. If this white man had not stopped, no one knows what would be your son's future."

The crowd began to become agitated, but in agreement with the Elder and Mongo. Another man yelled at the children, "You kids be quiet! Can't you see how important this is?"

Someone advised the parents, "Go quickly! Get some things so you can take your son to the hospital. God has helped you today."

Slowly, the father calmed, and asked more questions while his wife ran to the house. She returned with some needed items, and got in next to her son. Mongo and the elder climbed in, and Paul revved up the motor and pulled away.

Paul breathed a sigh of relief. "Thank you, Jesus. You got us through."

Night had fallen and the headlights showed the trail. Only the track was visible in the dense jungle. Suddenly, they came to the bridge that was being repaired. There was just one huge problem. There was no bridge! They looked at open water in front of them!!

"Oh no!" exclaimed Mongo. "They didn't finish!"

Paul stepped out of the vehicle with Mongo and the Elder, asking the woman to stay with her son. They saw the planks laid to one side of the embankment. Only two large logs spanned the stream from one bank to the other.

"I know what we can do!" said Paul. "We'll put some boards on so we can cross! Quick, take the end of this plank. I'll lift the other end."

Together, the three men reassembled the bridge plank-by-plank until there was enough support to drive across.

As they finished, some boys, who had been swimming in the water, came up and asked, "Are you military guys?"

"No," replied the Elder, "we just want to get across the stream!"

They got in and continued their journey.

When they arrived at the hospital, Paul went to Dr. Bob, an orthopedic surgeon. He said, "Bob, an accident seriously injured a boy's leg today. Please do all you can…but you should know this: He is the son of a village Chieftain! If the son can't walk out of this hospital on his own two legs, both of us will be in deep trouble!" Paul's statement was true. The only option was that the boy could walk home.

Thankfully, Dr. Bob specialized in such challenges. He had worked on more difficult cases in Vietnam.

Two weeks later the boy and his mother were dismissed from the hospital. They walked ten miles back home. During their hospital stay they heard the story of Jesus many times and hospital workers prayed with them. They knew that this accident was truly a "God thing."

A year later Pastor Paul was preaching in a nearby village. The mother came to hear about Jesus, and she brought Paul a thanksgiving gift of a stalk of fresh bananas because he had saved her son.

Paul never discovered who had been praying for him on that day, but he knew that God had answered someone's prayer because *"The prayer of a righteous person is powerful and effective"* (James 5:16).

THOUGHT QUESTIONS:
CHAPTER 9
FREAK ACCIDENT—A GOD MOMENT

Accidents are very frightening, especially when there aren't emergency specialists. But even in a place of danger, the Holy Spirit will use it for His purposes.

This story showed how important it is for us to pray for one another. If we know people working in cultures where the Gospel is not well known, we must faithfully pray for their protection.

1.   Acts 12:1-18—Describe how the prayer of the Christians was important? Memorize James 5:16.

2.   Whose thoughts did God reset in the story? How did He do it?

3.   Why is prayer so important to the life of the Christ-   follower?

4.   What changes will you make so that you have a stronger prayer life?

CHAPTER 10
WHAT IF SOMEONE DIES?

Kizu was deep in the Yombe forest. How would the students get the Good News to this remote village?

The Holy Spirit was touching many lives through the student ministries. Ten villages had been opened to the Gospel, and there was a small group of believers in each one.

One Friday morning, Paul was driving to the town of Tshela, he passed through the market where the ladies from the surrounding jungle towns brought their harvest to sell and trade. He saw a woman carrying a heavy basket on her back and a bundle on her head. She was walking toward the jungle trail that leads to Kizu.

He stopped, and his student, Ngoma, called to her, *"Mama! Mama!"*

She turned, and he motioned her to come.

Paul greeted her and then asked, "Do you live in Kizu?"

"Yes, Tata." She responded.

"Please forgive me, Mama," Paul began, "…but will you tell your chief that Pastor Paul would like to come for a short visit tomorrow?"

"Yes, Tata." she responded. "When?"

"Tomorrow when the sun is at early afternoon."

"Yes, Tata, I will," she promised. They watched her disappear into the jungle.

Paul and Ngoma left campus early Friday afternoon. They drove on the water-puddled road for about four miles, descended down over a log bridge and then, leaving the main road, they plunged into the jungle. The trail twisted through thick forest. Branches along the center of the path bumped the windshield and scraped the sides of the car. Trees blocked the sunshine, keeping the road dark. They drove through a small stream and up the other bank.

Suddenly, they broke through the jungle into an opening. Paul stopped and spoke to a boy who was nearby. "Greetings, my son. Please show us the Chieftain's house."

The boy turned his head towards the end of the row of houses and pointed with his lips and nose, "Over there, next to that big mango tree."

"Thank you." Paul and Ngoma responded together.

As they drove forward between two rows of huts, the boy ran beside the car waving, *"Mundele! Mundele!"* [White man! White man!].

They parked by the mango tree and walked toward the hut. There didn't appear to be anyone at home, so Ngoma called out while clapping his hands, *"koko, koko, koko! Tata Mfumu bwala!"* [knock knock! Mr. Village Chief!].

They stood and listened. A voice from behind the hut answered, "Inga, minu kaka! [Just me, I'm here!]" The man hurried around the house toward Paul and Ngoma.

As the two visitors approached, the Chieftain came directly to them, and knelt in front of Paul. He reached up for Paul's hand, "Welcome to my home, Pastor."

Nobody had ever knelt to greet Paul.

"Please...," Paul began, "...please stand, we are friends."

"Yes," corrected the chief, "...but you are special. Come and sit."

Paul wondered why he was special.

"Come, sit under my tree." The Chieftain pointed to three long-chairs in the shade.

Everyone sat down, relaxing in the chairs.

"Did the lady inform you that we would come today?" Paul asked.

"Yes, Tata Paul. She told me," he affirmed.

"Do you know what it is we want to talk about?" Paul asked.

"Yes...," he began, "you want to talk about bringing us the Voice of God."

Paul and Ngoma clicked their tongues with surprise, "How did you know that?" asked Ngoma.

"Oh, everyone in the Yombe jungle knows that when Pastor Paul comes with his students, it is to bring us the Voice of God," he stated as if it was a fact. And he panned the tops of the trees with his hand to show that all the forest people knew this.

"That's wonderful," began Paul. "My Father...," he continued with respect, "we come to you with the Voice of God. We want to assure you that we are not here to take your people away. Our students will come with only one purpose, to tell you about Jesus."

"Oh, we know," the Chief affirmed. "The ancestor taught us that one day someone would come with the Voice of God. We know that you will bring Him to us. That's what our people want," he affirmed, and then he asked, "When will you come?"

"Today is Friday," responded Paul. "May we begin tomorrow night?"

The Chieftain looked alarmed and shocked. Gazing again at the forest tree tops, he clicked his tongue and began to speak very carefully, "But, Pastor Paul, that won't do! What if someone in my village dies tonight and never hears the Voice of God? Then who will be responsible for his lost soul?"

Now it was Paul and Ngoma's turn to gasp! This was the first Chief to ask them such a question!

These people believe that the Chief holds the souls of all his villagers in his hand. If anyone dies and does not get to the village of the ancestors, it is believed that the chief will answer to God on judgment day. The Kizu Chieftain did not want any of his people to miss the Voice of God.

Paul looked at Ngoma. "Can your team be ready tonight?" he asked. "This means we'll be back in four hours."

Ngoma looked at his watch. "We'll be here!" he promised.

The Chieftain looked happy. "Good! I'll be sure everyone is ready," he promised.

As darkness fell on the village of Kizu, the people came together to hear the Story of Jesus' love and sacrifice for them. The students learned that when the Holy Spirit prepares someone to hear God's Voice, they must make the time to tell them, because the Lord *"... is patient with you, not wanting anyone to perish, but everyone to come to repentance"* (2 Peter 3:9).

God's Voice was speaking in the forest.

THOUGHT QUESTIONS:
CHAPTER 10
WHAT IF SOMEONE DIES?

What if someone dies without ever knowing that God loves them and that Jesus came to forgive their sins? There are many people in the world who have never heard about Jesus' love. This story told us about a village Chieftain who was very concerned that every one of his people would hear the Voice of God. He was not happy if someone died without knowing.

1.   Read Acts 16:6-10. Why did the Holy Spirit change the Apostle Paul's direction of missionary work? Memorize 2 Peter 3:9-- what does God not want people to do?

2.   How did the Holy Spirit use the Chieftain to reset Paul's thinking about coming to his village?

3.   How can you pray for people who haven't heard about Jesus? What can you do to help them hear about Him?

CHAPTER 11
A GIFT FOR MAMA

Sometimes less isn't best!

The old 4 x 4 had been sold. As a result, Paul traveled the jungle trails on a motorcycle while he waited for the new truck.

The motor bike seemed too small for Professor Mata to travel with Paul. Nevertheless, they squeezed together on the bike and rode down the jungle trails.

They were a perfect duo. Two times a month they traveled to remote villages to conduct a two-day training conference. They slept in the village huts, ate with the people, and worshiped with them.

The morning began at 5:30 a.m. when the host pastor called the trainees to early prayers.

After prayers and breakfast, everyone gathered in the central worship place for Bible teaching and training on subjects of how to study the Bible, how to share the Gospel, how to teach the Bible, personal finances and church history. By the end of the conference, the participants would identify the villages in their county where the Gospel was not yet known. Then, they appointed evangelists to begin visiting those hidden places.

Pastor Mata often taught lessons on Bible study and personal finances. However, as he taught about tithing, the Holy Spirit convinced him that he, as the teacher, should also be obedient to God's principle of tithing. But, if he tithed, he feared that he would not have enough to feed his growing family of six girls. As he studied, he became convinced that God takes care of those who put Him first (Malachi 3:10). He began giving the tithe and offerings, too. He didn't know that God was guiding him to an unsettling truth.

It is an African custom to give the guest a departure gift. On the last day of the conference, the village elders called Pastors Paul and Mata aside for a solemn presentation. Everyone gathered in a circle. In these ceremonies, there was usually one man standing in the center of the circle holding a goat on a leash.

The man would say, "It is our custom to thank the guest who comes to give us God's Voice. You have sacrificed much to come to us. We cannot repay you for your service, so we give you the best of what we have. This animal is our sacrifice to you. We want you to take this home with you and present it to your wife so she can see that when you came to our village, we took good care of you." He would then hand the leash to Pastor Paul.

Paul would show great appreciation and respond, "You are very gracious to us. We don't deserve anything that we are given. It all comes from God. We see that this animal is very strong and good. My Mama (meaning his wife, Marian!) will be very pleased to receive this. And if she could come with me, she would thank you very much. Thank you. May God bless you."

He would then hand the leash to Pastor Mata who would make another speech, very much like the first one. Pastor Mata would then hand the leash back to the village elder and asked that he please tie up the goat and put it in the vehicle. When they rode the motorcycle, a bamboo extension rack was tied to the back, and the unfortunate goat was attached to it.

The two professors came home with a goat or chicken every time. However, it was against the rules of the Bible School to keep living animals on campus. So, as soon as they drove up to Paul's house, the goat went out back and was butchered and his meat went into the freezer.

Paul told Pastor Mata, "That meat in the freezer is for you, too. Whenever your wife wants to feed your family, she should come and get a piece. You can have as much meat, every day, as you can eat."

And so Mrs. Mata came two or three times a week to get meat.

At the end of one school year Paul and Mata were counting the blessings of God.

Paul said, "Pastor, what did God do this year?"

Mata smiled big, "He gave us many important opportunities to share Jesus with people."

"Yes," responded Paul, "and what did you, Mata, learn from God this year?"

"I learned the importance of tithing, and how God wants me to give to Him what already belongs to Him."

"Did you notice," Pastor Paul continued "that this year you had meat for your family two or three times a week? It came from putting God first."

"Oh Yes!" Mata exclaimed. "Our family rarely eats meat! But this year, God blessed us every week. He is so wonderful, just like the Bible says, *"My God will meet all your needs…in Christ Jesus"* (Philippians 4:19).

God had reset Pastor Mata's idea about tithing. Everything we have comes from Him!

THOUGHT QUESTIONS:
CHAPTER 11
A GIFT FOR MAMA

The things we own can keep us from obeying Him. Bible authors teach many lessons about the importance of being generous. They teach that everything we have as followers of Jesus belongs to Him, and we are His managers of what we own. This story showed us how important it is to trust God with our possessions.

1. Read 2 Corinthians 9:6-11—What is God's promise in these verses to those who show an attitude of generous giving for God's work? Memorize Philippians 4:19.

2. What did the Holy Spirit teach Pastor Mata that reset his ideas about money?

3. What must you do to be a generous person who shares what God gives you? What ways can you share?

CHAPTER 12
AN EPILEPTIC SEIZURE!

The pastor at Kami invited Paul to speak at a quarterly conference. Fortunately, Paul did not know the importance of the event or he would have felt very intimidated. It would be his first time to preach in the Kikongo language.

He prepared a message that taught how the Communion Celebration reminds us of the death and resurrection of Jesus. To illustrate the suffering of Jesus on the cross, he asked Mongo to make a crown of thorns from a jungle vine. They also made a whip that looked like the one used to scourge Jesus.

Everything was set: the message, the visual objects and the plan.

Sunday arrived. Mongo and Paul drove the red-rutty clay road to Kami. It took almost ninety minutes to drive the twenty miles. When they drove into the village, they saw the roadway lined with palm branches to greet the guests. The women were dressed in colorful robes. There were so many people in the village that one could hardly pass through the crowds to reach the church.

A choir in colorful robes marched and sang their way to the front of the worship center. The pastors and church board members mounted the platform and sat in assigned seats, placing Paul at the center. Then, the congregation entered. People were sitting in every window! Three hundred people squeezed into a sanctuary that might seat one hundred in America. Nobody noticed that the room was smothering hot as they sang, clapped and prayed.

After two hours of songs, including a forty-five-minute march offering, the Master of Ceremonies introduced Paul with a fifteen-minute description of his background, credentials and experience. Paul stepped nervously to the podium holding his sermon manuscript. This was the first full-length sermon he preached in the native language. He thought everything was in order.

"Mbot'eno!" he greeted them.

"Mbote!" they called back so loud that the roof tins rattled.

Paul slowly began reading from the carefully written manuscript. He wanted every word and gesture to be clearly understood. As his message continued the words flowed faster. When he came to the teaching about the suffering of Jesus, he stepped down from the platform so he could reach out and touch the people in the front row.

"Soldiers took a crown of thorns like this one...," he began, as he held up the crown, "and they did not put this on his head gently. The soldiers were angry that they had to do this. They made sure that Jesus suffered. One put this on Jesus' head and pushed down hard so it wouldn't fall off. These thorns poked into His skin and flesh." Paul tried to imitate what it must have looked like.

The people were completely silent. Some were holding their breath.

"Then, a soldier took a whip like this one." He held up a whip made of jungle vines. "They tied Jesus to a pole with his arms stretched up so that his skin on the back was tight." Some listeners were holding their hand in front of their mouth in horror.

Paul continued, "The law said that the punishment was forty lashes on His back. But the Jewish law required that they show grace and mercy to the criminal. So, they only lashed Him thirty-nine times!"

Paul looked at the people, "So now, as I lash the floor, count with me." He struck the floor, "One...two...three." The people counted in unison after each strike. When they reached ten, their voices began to fade and then they were quiet. A woman in the front row began to weep.

Paul stopped whipping the floor and returned to the podium. "This," he continued, "is what Jesus suffered for our sins!" He paused.

"When we take this cup and this bread in Communion, it reminds us that Jesus completely removed sin from us—He paid the highest price with His life."

BAM! SMASH!

It was the sound of someone falling on the cement floor.

People gasped. Many stood, turning and looking back to where a man lay on the floor, thrown down by a grand mal epileptic seizure! Everyone was talking and fearful because they believe that seizures are caused by demons, not an illness.

Dr. Joseph left the platform and went through the crowd to the man.

Paul went to the choir master, "Start your song to draw people back."

They began to sing as loudly as their voices could rise in rhythm to drums and tambourines.

Some men lifted the sick man and took him out the back door. The crowd separated like two waves.

The choir was singing with all their energy about Jesus who healed the blind man and made his vision change from seeing trees to seeing people.

The crowd settled down, Paul gathered his thoughts, prayed and then finished the message.

God visited His people that day. Many found peace in Christ, and the sick man was taken to the hospital to receive help for his illness.

Paul went home tired and thankful that "...*the Word of God is living and active. Sharper than a double-edged sword...*" (Hebrews 4:12). All of his best preparation was no match for what God wanted to do when he taught the Bible.

THOUGHT QUESTIONS:
CHAPTER 12
AN EPILEPTIC SIEZURE!

Ever since Mr. Gutenberg printed the first Bible, it has been the most desired book in the world. Even some people who aren't followers of Jesus want to read the Bible. When the Bible is taught, people learn about God and about themselves.

God told the prophet Isaiah and many others that God's Word will always accomplish God's goal of changing a life. This is why it is so important for us to pay attention to the Word of God, His Bible.

1.   Read Isaiah 55:6-11—What does God promise that His Word will do? Memorize Hebrews 4:12.

2.   Why do you think that the epileptic seizure did not stop the people from hearing and understanding the Bible teaching in this story?

3.   What kind of things did Paul and other worship leaders do to keep people focused on worship?

4.   In what ways are you learning God's Word and hiding it in your heart so that it will work in you?

CHAPTER 13
FIVE IN THREE

Paul and Nathan left home in a small pick-up truck. They didn't know that their mechanic had forgotten something. No one should travel without a good spare tire!

Bad luck was about to poke holes in a good weekend!

Nathan was excited! He would be traveling with his father for a three-day tour of speaking in village churches. Nathan, in second grade had recently arrived home for Christmas break. He had been living in a dorm for the past four months. Now, he could room with brother Jayson, and he enjoy six weeks without any homework. Staying in the village was a special treat, and traveling with just Dad was even better.

He loaded his backpack with clothing, some matchbox cars and his Bible.

They traveled north on the paved highway through the villages in the Yombe forest, slowing to avoid goats, and swerving to miss chickens on the road. As they rolled through villages, children ran along and waved at the passing truck. When they saw Nathan they screamed with delight, *"Mwan'a mundele!"* [white child!] and they pointed and waved at the same time.

Then it happened! Ten miles from Tshela, their destination, a rear tire went flat. Paul was perplexed; "We just put new tires on this thing! Why the flat?" They got out and watched the tire gasp the last breath of air.

"Do we have a spare?" asked Nathan.

"We are supposed to have one. Ngoma, our mechanic, put one in when we got new tires."

They took out the jack and lifted the flat tire off the ground. They quickly unscrewed the lug nuts and removed it. Then, they took out the spare tire. Paul thought it looked funny … but it wasn't funny at all! It was flat!

"Now what do we do?" wondered Paul.

"There is no place to fix it in the jungle," said Nathan, "and we don't have a pump."

"I know what we do first." said Paul, "Let's sit down and pray."

They sat down by the road and prayed. "Jesus, we don't know how this can be fixed, but please send another truck, or something."

"Amen."

They looked up and a man on a bike was approaching them. "Abwe?" he asked, "What happened?"

Paul looked up, *"Mbote Tata!"* [Greetings, mister]. "Our tire went flat and the spare is also flat, and we don't have tools to fix it." He pointed at the flat tires.

The man was silent for a moment. "Oh…" he began. "In the next village is a young man who fixes bike tires. Maybe he fixes truck tires, too. I can take this flat to him and maybe he can fix it."

"Ngitukulu! [Amazing!]" exclaimed Paul. "We will tie this tire to your bike rack, and here is some money to pay him."

The man took the tire and money and peddled down the road, whistling joyfully.

"Will he bring back the tire, Daddy?" Nathan asked a bit worried. "Sometimes selling a tire brings extra money."

"I hope so." Paul answered.

"Well," Nathan mused, "at least he can't use our tire as a spare on his bike!"

One hour later Nathan saw the man coming down the road. He was singing as he came, and carrying the tire!

They remounted it and put the tools away. Paul gave the angel-in-disguise a gift of money for his work, and he rode off into the forest singing. Paul and Nathan continued their journey to Tshela, hoping there would be no more problems.

They arrived at Pastor Silas' house in time for dinner. He greeted them with a big smile. "Man alive!" he said in English. "Nice to see you!" Pastor Silas liked English expressions.

His wife welcomed them to her table. They ate a healthy meal of rice with chicken in palm oil gravy, rich spinach cooked in palm oil and mangos for dessert.

Paul told Silas about their flat tires and asked if the spare could be fixed before leaving for the night meeting. Pastor Silas called in a friend who took the tire.

After the meal, everyone prayed again, thanking God for providing safety and help in time of need. They also prayed that people would respond to the Holy Spirit that night.

The choir climbed into the back of the pickup with Nathan. Pastor Silas and Paul took the seat in the cab. Just before they drove away, the repaired spare tire was returned to the back of the truck.

The choir sang loudly as they bounced over dirt roads and ruts, through villages and more forest. They splashed through the last puddle before the destination; and suddenly Paul felt a strange mushiness in the steering. He pulled over, parked and heard a hissing sound: "SSSSSSSSSSSS".

One of the singers jumped out and pointed to the front tire, "Pastor, this tire is singing, too!"

Paul put his hand to the tire rim. He felt air leaking very quickly. "We'll put on a different one after the meeting," he commented.

That evening more than two hundred people came from the surrounding villages to hear the message about Jesus who forgives our sins. They danced with the choir music. As Paul spoke, they clicked their tongues in agreement and shook their heads saying, *"makedika, makedika!* [True words, true words]."

At the conclusion, Pastor Silas asked, "Who would like to ask Jesus to forgive your sins? Remember, only Jesus can do it."

Several people stood to pray with Pastor Silas, "Jesus, forgive me because I am a sinner," they declared. The pastor led them with a prayer that they repeated after him, "Jesus, forgive me. I have sinned against you. I trust your death and resurrection as the only sacrifice that can clean my sinful heart. I trust you, Jesus, to guide me. I want to obey you and your words. Ameni!"

They concluded and the choir returned to the truck—with a flat front tire!

Many hands make work easy—and the tire was quickly changed. They bounced back to the church, singing and praising God.

Everyone turned in for bed after a cup of sweet tea.

They were awakened at 6:00 am to the sound of the talking drum calling everyone to early morning prayers. The sun was coming up over the hill.

There was knocking at the door. "Pastor Paul! Are you awake?" asked Pastor Silas.

"Yes, we are coming!" responded Paul.

Nathan followed as they walked to the large church for prayers. After greeting everyone, they walked by the truck to the house. Nathan looked at the truck that was leaning to one side.

"Daddy! We have another flat tire!" he exclaimed. "I think we have a flat tire sickness!" he sighed.

The tire was removed, along with last night's flat, and sent to the repairman.

Saturday night found them bouncing on another jungle road to a different village. The sky was so clear they could see millions of stars in the Milky Way galaxy.

"See…," said Nathan, "there is Orion's belt!"

"Isn't it neat to see what God created?" Paul commented, "and if He can make a sky that big and pretty, do you suppose He can take care of us, too?" he asked.

"Yup! Maybe our tires, too!" answered Nate.

Several hundred people came to the meeting. They sat on mats and stools. Children brought pieces of firewood on their heads. They sang. They prayed earnestly. After Paul's message, Pastor Silas invited people to receive forgiveness. Like the first night, many people stood and declared their desire to follow Jesus.

After a special meal with the village Chieftain, they returned to the pickup and discovered that it was again leaning to one side. Nathan saw it first, "Dad, another one!" and he pointed.

"How many does that make now?" asked Paul.

Nate began to count on his fingers, "on the road, last night, this morning, and now—that makes four!" he declared.

"What about the spare tire?" he asked.

"Oh!" said Nate, "That makes five in three days."

"I hope the flat tire sickness goes away pretty soon," added Paul.

The next day was Sunday—the biggest worship day of the week. Nearly a thousand people came for a special day of worship, Holy Communion and to meet friends. Ladies were cooking rice in huge pots over open fires. Some men were butchering the honorary goat. Others were sweeping the yard. Everything had to be just right for this important day.

The bell rang, announcing the time to enter the worship center. Worshipers packed in so tight they couldn't wiggle. Teenage boys sat in the open windows. Babies stayed with mama. Four choirs squeezed around the platform.

People waved and danced to the throb of music. Worshiping God is an exciting event.

After ninety minutes, the elders announced the march offering. The women would compete against the men. The purpose of this gala event was to make giving a hilarious and fun worship experience.

As the music and drums thumped the rhythm, people began to sing and pick up the march tempo. The ladies danced in perfect unison, waving yellow bandannas in the air, and swaying in perfect rhythm. Some ladies had banana stalks or potatoes on their heads. They danced keeping a perfect balance, and nothing fell off their heads.

Then, the men and boys took their turn, weaving through the crowd from the entrance to the platform. They waved money in the air, dancing in rhythm to songs. Some men carried a chicken or a rabbit. They dropped their gift in the plate, or placed goods on the food stack. No one wanted to lose this contest!

Pastor Silas, Paul and Nathan were watching from the platform. It was noon, and the offering wasn't ending any time soon. Pastor Silas leaned over to Paul, "Let's go have dinner! Follow me."

He stood, and Paul and Nathan followed. They crossed the yard to the house where they sat down to a full meal of rice, sauce and goat cooked in palm oil, and beans. Everyone took their time eating.

After a banana dessert, Silas prayed to thank God for their good meal. He stood up, and Paul and Nate followed him back to the sanctuary where the music and offering were still throbbing.

Finally, the marchers sat down. The music pastor led in a hymn while the elders counted the offering. After a second hymn, the treasurer stood up to announce the total.

"This is what we gave to God today. The women gave 20,045 Zaires. The men gave 20,100 Zaires and the women brought all of these potatoes and bananas." He pointed to the piles.

Then he asked, "Are we happy with the results?"

The men yelled back, "Yes!"

The women cried, "NO! You didn't count the potatoes and rice and bananas!"

The Elder responded, "Next time we'll do better!" He prayed for the offering and they announced that Pastor Paul would now give the message.

After the greeting, Paul began, "We have given generously to our God today because we are thankful to Him for His most wonderful gift, that is Jesus…" He continued to describe how God loved the world so much that He sent His only begotten Son, Jesus.

Pastor Silas invited people to dedicate themselves to Jesus so they, too, could experience His love. Many people came to Jesus that day.

As Paul and Nathan drove home to Boma, they knew that God had blessed the weekend. They also realized that when the Holy Spirit is going to do something special the Enemy of our souls, Satan, puts up a fuss to discourage or even poke holes in what the Spirit comes to do—such as five flat tires in three days!

When they arrived home, they talked about the things that the Spirit did for people. Paul commented, "We saw how our '…*help comes from the Lord, the Maker of heaven and earth… The Lord watches over us*'" (Psalm 121:2, 5).

"Yes…," responded Nathan, "when our plan ends—God's plan begins."

THOUGHT QUESTIONS:
CHAPTER 13
FIVE IN THREE

When was the last time your car had a flat tire? I wonder if you were frustrated because it made you take a lot of extra time. What if you had five flat tires in one trip in places where flats are hard to fix? That could be very discouraging. This story showed us that even with a flat tire, you can see God's presence.

1.   Read Psalms 121—What does God promise to those who look to Him for their help? Memorize Psalm 121:1-2.

2.   Paul was not prepared for five flats in three days. In spite of that, what different things did God prepare so that Paul and Nathan were able to take the Gospel to these villages?

3.   What are some ways that you completely depend on God, even when things seem to go wrong?

CHAPTER 14
I KILLED MY BABY!

Paul didn't know what surprise the host pastor planned.

Dry season had come with cool weather and bright moonlit nights. It was the time when Christians went to the streets and fields to invite friends to hear the Story of Jesus. Pastors traveled to other parishes to serve as guest evangelists for ten days. Paul was invited to Kangu, a large town on the main highway to the jungle region.

"Koko, Koko," Pastor Masiala called at the front door.

"Come in," invited Pastor Paul.

As they talked about next week, Paul asked, "What will we do?"

The answer was like music to his ears!

"Pastor Paul...," he began, "if we are going to talk to people who don't know about Jesus, then we need to go to them. So, when you come to Kangu, we will not have any meeting in the church building. Instead, we are going into the streets and yards."

"That's wonderful!" responded Pastor Paul. It was exactly what he had hoped for since it seemed strange to expect someone who never comes to church to enter the door just for a special meeting. It is better to go to them.

Paul drove to Kangu for the special week. He stayed with Pastor Masiala and his wife. Every meeting was different.

Monday night, they went to the home of a Christian family and gathered in the front lawn. As people began to come with their friends, the yard soon filled with excitement. Suddenly, a noisy band from next door interrupted.

"What's that?" asked the pastor.

"Oh," responded a church Elder, "it's the K-sect. They decided to have band practice tonight. Sadly, they want to do it right next to us and at the same time."

"Not a problem!" observed Pastor Masiala. He called over the host in whose yard they were meeting. "Brother, do you know those people next door?"

"Yes," he replied.

"Is there something we can do so that their band practice won't interrupt our meeting?" Pastor asked.

"Sure! I'll go talk to them." the man volunteered.

He went next door and explained to the bandleader, "We have a meeting tonight in our yard. Many people are coming to hear a special speaker. Would you like to come and join us…and practice your songs after the meeting?"

The bandleader was interested, "Sure, we'll do that!" They put down their instruments and came to the meeting to hear the true story about Jesus. That night many people trusted Jesus as their Savior.

On Wednesday, the congregation moved to a major intersection where two state highways come together. The pastor and worship leaders used an elevated storefront as their platform.

People gathered as the songs began. They came from the marketplace, and from their houses carrying their stools, chairs and mats. Soon several hundred people were seated in the intersection. If a vehicle came to the intersection, it stopped—they had no choice. Fortunately, there were very few vehicles, because people don't travel after dark in that part of Africa. Trucks stopped, and the passengers joined the event.

After the service, the pastor asked for people to come to the platform to receive forgiveness in Jesus. Many came. One young girl wanted to talk with Pastor Paul. She confessed a life of sleeping with men whom she had not married. She was very remorseful as she confessed what she had done.

"Pastor, I don't know if Jesus can forgive me," she wept. "I got pregnant and did not want the baby, so I had an abortion. Even though I am free from the baby, I am a slave to my shame. I killed my baby! … Can God forgive me?" She couldn't look up. Her burden of shame was too heavy.

Pastor Paul said, "Tonight, we talked about the moment that Jesus became the sacrifice for our sin…all of us and all of our sin. But there was a bandit who was on a cross next to Jesus. He had killed many people. Just before he died, he asked Jesus to forgive him, and what did Jesus do?"

"He forgave the bandit," she responded.

"Can Jesus do this for you, too?" Paul asked.

"Yes, He can, I think." She responded, still not sure

"The Apostle wrote a word of comfort for you," Paul added, "He said that *'if we confess our sins, He [Jesus] is faithful and just and will forgive us our sins…'* (1 John 1:9). This truth is for you. Can you hold to it?"

"I will," she agreed.

They prayed together and she went home, free in her soul, knowing God had lifted her burden.

THOUGHT QUESTIONS:
CHAPTER 14
I KILLED MY BABY!

When we take the Good News to people who need it, they want Jesus' help, but we must go to people who need to hear the Good News. This story told how a pastor took Paul to places and people who needed to hear about Jesus. As a result, many people heard and received Jesus' love.

1.   Read John 8:1-11—Describe what we must do when we want Jesus to forgive us. Memorize 1 John 1:9.

2.   What are the different ways that Jesus showed his forgiveness to people during this week of meetings?

3.   Why was it so important that this girl should know that Jesus could forgive her?

4.   What is there in your life that you need to ask Jesus to forgive? Please pray now and ask Him to forgive you, and trust the promise of 1 John 1:9.

INTERLUDE

The British Air jet, a Boeing 747, lifted up from Kinshasa, (Congo) airport on its way to London. Paul and Marian looked out the window watching the nightlights darken. They had been in the Congo for ten years. In their hearts, they knew that many people had learned how to tell The Story; many students were serving in parts of the Congo where there was very little knowledge of Jesus. Villages and city boroughs had chapels, and new followers were telling neighbors about Jesus.

The Holy Spirit did wonderful acts.

However, they had a feeling deep inside that told them that something new was coming. They wondered what it would be, but they didn't talk about it at that moment because it seemed strange, and a little sad, to be leaving the Congo.

Before Paul and Marian went to the Congo, they had given their lives to serve Jesus wherever He sent them. The Holy Spirit promised that He would always tell them when the next opportunity was coming. After ten years in the Congo, where would He send them next?

As they flew through the night over Africa, they watched the moonlight reflect off the Sahara Desert far below, and they marveled at the bigness of God. They were reminded of His promise, *"Never will I leave you; never will I forsake you"* (Hebrews 13:5). Even their magnificent God cared about them! He doesn't forget his children!

Note: The Keidels were transferred from the Congo to the Republic of Guinea in West Africa where they taught at a Bible school that trained young men and women to lead churches. The stories that follow illustrate God's gentle resetting of lives in a country that is 85% Muslim. Many names and places have been changed to protect the Christians.

CHAPTER 15
NOBODY TO MEET THEM!

Conakry, Guinea

One year later, an Air France A-350 jet was banking over the Bay of Guinea, descending into the small Conakry International Airport. Marian and Paul watched the city lights twinkling brighter as they landed.

They wondered why the Holy Spirit was leading them to Guinea? What would their ministry be like in this new country? Would it be like the Congo? They had left Congo to come to another country that they had never seen.

The vast majority of people in Guinea are followers of Islam. Islam had declared a jihad [Holy War] on the people of Guinea in the 18th Century. Their goal had been to convert all of the eleven million people of this nation to Allah, the God of Islam. After two hundred years, more than 85% of the men and women of Guinea bowed their heads to the ground.

Five times each day, the Muslim people of Guinea stopped what they were doing, knelt on their prayer rugs looking toward Mecca and declared, "There is no God but Allah, and Mohammed is his prophet."

The Airbus touched down on the single cement landing strip and came to a quick halt in front of the reception building. Passengers began moving forward in the aisle, leaving the plane down the steps to the ground. As they entered the immigration area, a crowd reached out to greet them and grab their papers. Paul and Marian ignored all the grabbers and walked straight to a table where a friendly man stamped their passports and pointed to the luggage claim area.

Soon, their four suitcases came through, and they went to customs. A soldier interrogated them, "Who are you? What do you have to claim?"

Paul wondered what all he would ask about, but decided to wait. "We are here to work for the Protestant Church. We have our belongings that we will use for four years." He declared.

The man looked at them. He didn't understand.

Paul found a printed tract that explained the story of Jesus. He handed it to the Muslim man and explained, "This tells you what we do."

The man looked at it, and then gruffly pushed it back to Paul. "Move on!" he ordered.

Paul and Marian picked up their belongings and moved quickly before the soldier might change his mind. They stepped into the greeting area that was filled with a huge crowd of disorganized people demanding, "Taxi! Taxi!" People tried to grab their bags. Young boys forcefully shined their shoes and demanded payment.

Paul tried to see above the crowd to find a recognizable face, but saw no one.

"Do you see anyone?" asked Marian.

"No," he answered. "I guess we wait." They felt very much alone.

Finally, Paul saw a sign high on a wall. It said: "TELEPHONE".

"There...," Paul pointed. "I'll see if I can call someone."

Marian moved through the crowd toward a corner with the suitcases, while Paul forced through to the telephone. He saw a man sitting behind the desk reading a magazine.

"Bonjour," [Good day] Paul greeted him across the desk top. "May I call my friend on the phone?"

"Sure, no problem." He responded, "What is the number?"

"I don't know!" Paul said. "Do you have a phone book?"

The man looked perplexed. "What is a phone book?" he asked.

Paul wondered how he would describe a phone book. "It's a book that has lists of peoples' names and their phone numbers."

"Oh, I know!" the man recognized what Paul needed. He handed him a piece of cardboard the size of typing paper. "Here is the list!" he announced.

Paul took the cardboard and scrutinized the fifteen names scribbled in confused disorder. He did not find the name he wanted. "Thank you," he said as he handed it back.

He pushed through the crowd to Marian wondering what to do next.

"Did you call them?" Marian asked.

"No, all he has is a piece of cardboard with some names on it. I guess we wait."

"Paul…Marian…!" someone was calling to them over the crowd. They looked over the people and saw a white hand waving above the African faces. It was Mel, their host.

"I'm sorry I'm late." he apologized. "I came when the plane was supposed to land, and they said it would be much later. So, I went home; and instead, it came on time. WAWA! [West Africa Wins Again]." Mel announced.

That evening, after a good meal and much conversation, they thanked God for new friends. They went to sleep knowing that the Almighty One, the God of Israel, was looking out for them. They learned to trust Him in everything, putting Him first. God would prove many times over that when they trusted Him, *"He will make their paths straight"* (Proverbs 3:6).

THOUGHT QUESTIONS:
CHAPTER 15
NOBODY MET THEM!

What happens when we are in a place where we don't know anyone?

Paul and Marian moved from Congo to Guinea. Although this was still in Africa, they were 3000 miles from Congo, but they were not alone. God, who sent them, also went with them just like He promised. This story showed how God directs our pathways, as He did for Paul & Marian.

1.   Read Proverbs 3:5-6—What must happen that God will direct your pathways? Memorize Proverbs 3:5-6.

2.   In what way did God watch out for Paul and Marian when they traveled to Guinea?

3.   What are the ways that you can trust in God's faithfulness when your plans don't go exactly right?

CHAPTER 16
TELEKORO—UNDER THE SON

It was early December, and Nathan and Jayson had come to Guinea for Christmas holiday. The family traveled together to Telekoro Bible Institute. It took them twelve hours to cover 300 miles

They wound through the Futa mountains, and then across the prairie on ruined pavement covered with dust. They were happy to arrive at their new home after dark, but surprised when they looked in a mirror. The dust from the road had stuck to their skin so they were either dark brown or red. As water from a bucket shower washed them, dirt water rolled off their bodies.

After a hearty dinner prepared by their new neighbors, they went to bed. Telekoro[4] was so remote on the Guinea prairie that only night sounds and total darkness put them to sleep.

At breakfast, Paul announced to the boys, "Let's explore the prairie!"

"Where are we going?" asked Jayson.

"We'll cross the rice paddies and see the river and small forest," Paul said.

They followed a narrow trail down to the rice fields. After walking a half-mile, they came to the sandy bank of the river Nyanda. The water was clear and waist deep. The boys jumped in and enjoyed the cool water in the warm air. Paul saw movement on the riverbank. A white and yellow snake, eight feet long, slithered into a large hole! He warned the boys, "Watch the movement around you. There is a big snake in a hole over there." He pointed to it.

The boys splashed and made noise to keep the snake away. After cooling down, they walked back across the prairie and the rice paddies to a small, polluted pond.

A student told them, "There are fish in there, but they are too small to eat."

---

[4] Telekoro means "under the sun", however, the missionaries and students understood it to mean "under the Son or Light" as a reference to Jesus.

"How big?" asked Nate.

"Like this," and he showed his little finger, "and they bite." He added.

The boys moved on.

That evening as they prayed together, they thanked God for bringing them to this place where they could say *"Every good and perfect gift is from above"* (James 1:17).

This promise would be tested many times during the coming years.

THOUGHT QUESTIONS:
CHAPTER 16
TELEKORO—UNDER THE SON

Paul and Marian moved to a new place where they didn't know anyone. They didn't know what living would be like, but they went, knowing that God always fulfills his promise to be a God who gives good and joy to those who obey and follow Him.

1.   Read James 1:16-18. Memorize James 1:17.

2.   What are some of the blessings and gifts that Paul and Marian discovered when they moved to their new home in Guinea?

3.   Why do you think it is important for you to count every gift as God's perfect gift to you?

4.   Count your blessings and see how many good and perfect gifts God has given you—list them (use extra paper, if necessary !!!)

CHAPTER 17
KILLER MALARIA!

The boys had returned to school in January after six weeks of holiday. Swimming in the Nyanda River and exploring the prairie had ended.

Now, they studied at the school for international workers' children: the "MK School" in Bouaké, Cote d'Ivoire (Ivory Coast). The fun part of school was that they could live with their friends. Sometimes, they referred to the school as the International Christian Academy (ICA), a yearlong summer camp of class time and soccer.

Paul and Marian finally had time to visit the boys at their school. But, they didn't know that a malaria-infected mosquito had already bitten Paul. The deadly disease was quietly spreading in his blood. The boys were anticipating a visit from their parents, not knowing how ill their father would become.

Paul and Marian left Telekoro early in the morning when it was cool. They drove their 4 x 4 across prairie and through the chimpanzee forests of Mount Nimba. They crossed a swift river where only a steel cable kept the ferry from being swept downstream.

After a night at a guest home, they drove another full day to ICA. The boys left campus to stay the weekend with their parents. They swam in the city pool, played soccer, went to the ice-cream shop and shared school stories together.

By Saturday afternoon Paul felt feverish, and he had a severe pain in the small of his back. It hurt so bad he had to lie down, but lying down made it hurt more. He couldn't find any relief standing, sitting or lying down.

By Sunday, his fever had reached 101 with a migraine headache. He knew it was malaria. This had happened many times since Paul's childhood. He swallowed the bitter malaria meds that always killed the parasite. Usually, the medication took effect within an hour, the headache would recede and the fever drop. But this time nothing changed!

He tried to sleep, but found no comfort. His temperature rose above 103, and he was sweating profusely. Then, suddenly it dropped and he was freezing. He knew this was the malaria cycle.

After twenty-four hours of misery, he took a different drug. His body had calmed enough for them to travel to another town to stay with friends. But, as soon as they completed the drive, his fever spiked up again. After two days, he felt much worse.

This time he took a "miracle drug" advertised as a sure cure. Six hours later his fever went very high and he could not keep fluids down.

Marian was alarmed. She and their hosts took him to a local doctor. Blood was drawn and tests showed that all the different drugs taken had done nothing to kill the malaria. The parasite count was extremely high, and it was the deadly breed that kills a half million people in Africa every year— more than any other illness or war.

The doctor looked at the test results and said, "You did what most white people do. You panicked and took all of this medicine. You must wait till you take the second dose and the illness will go away."

With very little hope, they returned to the house. Paul could not take the second dose for seven days. The week seemed endless with long nights and slow days! His fever climbed and dropped; profuse sweats were followed by freezing chills; severe headache and weakness followed, and he could not sleep nor could he eat. He could only keep down water. He was losing weight at an astounding rate!

Day seven came and he took the second dose of the miracle drug, but exactly six hours later his fever went very high. Now, nothing stayed in his stomach, not even water. He was quickly losing strength and dehydrating.

The mosquito bite was killing him! Everyone was gravely concerned.

Marian, with Craig and Marilyn, the host family, took counsel. They decided that Paul needed a trustworthy doctor. Craig called the Baptist mission hospital, six hours and 300 miles away. The response was immediate, "Bring him today quickly!"

Everyone gathered around Paul. Craig anointed him with oil, as it is written in James 5:13-14, "...and let them pray over him, anointing him with oil in the name of the Lord..." Paul felt a calm come over his body. He tried drinking some water, and this time it stayed down.

They loaded their bags with a mattress on top into the vehicle. Marian walked Paul to the car and he climbed in, lying down on the pad. Marian and Marilynn sat in front to drive to Ferkessédougou Hospital—six hours away. As they drove, they kept the windows open so the hot sun would not bake them in an oven. There was no air conditioning.

During the trip, Paul rested and drank water. God was answering their prayers. He was able to keep liquids down.

It was dark when they drove onto the hospital campus. They were directed to a nearby bungalow where Paul slowly walked to his bed. He was so weak now he could hardly take steps or speak.

The doctor came in, looked at him, and said, "I'm starting treatment now. I know what you have, and we will take tests later."

A nurse inserted the needle and started IV fluids, into which she added quinine. The fluids passed into his arm. In less than an hour, the fever dropped to normal temperature, and the headache stopped. The doctor had found a way to stop a malaria that is resistant to drugs.

This was the first time Paul came close to death, but it would not to be the last!

After an additional two months of recuperation, Paul was able to leave the hospital. He and Marian could finally drive back to Guinea. They took four days to make the return trip home, but the effects of the malaria continued, even though there was no malaria parasite in his body.

Still, something was not right about Paul's health.

He would be teaching a class, or sitting in a meeting, and, without warning, all his strength and energy disappeared. It felt like a fan being unplugged. When this happened, Paul had to lie down immediately.

He did not know that the culprit was a different parasite he had swallowed in a Congo village, six years before. It had multiplied inside him; and now his immune system was weakened by the malaria attack.

A year later, Paul was in Ouagadougou, Burkina Faso for a meeting. Suddenly he felt like the unplugged fan. He had to go to his room.

While he rested and prayed, the Holy Spirit said to him, "Paul, I want you to ask the men to anoint you and pray for you."

Paul argued, "How many times have I done this?"

The Spirit spoke again, "This is the last time you will ask for healing for this illness. Ask them tonight."

Paul obeyed the Spirit's instruction. That evening the men anointed Paul and prayed for him. He slept well that night. The next day he felt strong again. He traveled to the United States enduring the next thirty-six hours with very little sleep. But he did not lose strength. James wrote, *"and the prayer of faith will save the sick man"* (James 5:15).

This was the last time that special prayer was made for this illness. God came quietly to heal.

THOUGHT QUESTIONS:
CHAPTER 17
KILLER MALARIA!

Big problems sometimes come from little or unnoticed things. Telekoro is a school campus surrounded by rice patties. Mosquitoes thrive in swamps, and these mosquitoes were very dangerous because they carry malaria.

1.   Read James 5:13-18—What different ways are described in these verses of James that invite God to intervene (come to our help)? Memorize James 5:15.

2.   In what different ways did God intervene when Paul nearly died of malaria?

3.   According to the Bible verses you read, what should you do first when you find yourself in very frightening health circumstances?

CHAPTER 18
SURROUNDED BY ANGELS

Joseph was at the door. "Pastor Paul, I caught a thief!"

Paul came to the door. "What happened?" he asked, seeing a man with Joseph.

"I came to the motor room to start the generator and I found him taking diesel fuel. I will take him to the Director."

"Good! Thank you." Paul responded. "Let's wait and see what the school Director will do."

More than two hours passed. It was time to turn off the generator when a car pulled up to the house. The Director came in and sat down.

"Good evening…," Paul said, "…what happened?"

The Director took a deep breath and began to explain. "The man that Joseph caught is from the village of Kedou.

"I took him to the Chieftain, the leader of this man's clan. The Chief received us.

Then I told him, 'This man was caught stealing diesel fuel at the Bible School, so I have brought him to you.'

"The Chieftain became very angry and spoke to the man with strong words, 'Here you are, a grown man with a wife and a child. Why do you do something so stupid when you have the whole clan here to help you?'

"The Chief explained, 'Let me tell you something. I opposed the Bible School when it began many years ago. My father gave the land to the Christians to develop, but I was very angry. Since I was going to be the Chief, I already had great spirit powers. I made a blood sacrifice and called on my spirits. I ordered them to go to that school of Jesus people and do harm to them.

'The next morning in my prayers with the demons, they admitted that they did nothing the night before because they were afraid. So, I made a greater sacrifice and sent them a second time. And again, they returned without doing any harm.

'I asked them why they did nothing, because they are powerful spirits.

'They told me that both times when they arrived at the edge of the campus the whole property was surrounded by bright spirit-like people that were very powerful. They were protecting that place and my spirits could not get past them.'

"The Chief continued, 'Then I knew that the Name of Jesus is more powerful than my demons. That day I decided to give up my demon powers and to follow Jesus.'

"The Chief finished his story and turned to the ashamed thief. 'You dared to cross over that boundary that is protected by angels. Do you recognize your mistake?'

"The man was repentant."

The Director continued, "I've lived here for ten years, but this is the first time I heard the Chief's story! It's amazing!"

"Yes," responded Paul, "we are protected. Elijah taught his servant, *'Those who are with us are more than those who are with them'* (2 Kings 6:16). We don't know what we don't see."

THOUGHT QUESTIONS:
CHAPTER 18
SURROUNDED BY ANGELS

God's protection is always amazing, even when we aren't aware of it. The village Chieftain discovered a big surprise when he tried to put a curse on the Christians living at Telekoro. His discovery was so big that he changed his mind about the power of Jesus and became a follower of Jesus. This change represented a huge upset that reset his thinking.

1.   Read Psalm 34:1-7—Who does the Angel of the Lord protect? Why does He choose to protect these people? Memorize Psalm 34:7.

2.   Why was the Chieftain so unhappy with the young thief?

3.   What did the Chieftain's story tell the Director and Paul about the place where they lived?

4.   What kind of life must you live so that the Angel of the Lord will guard you?

CHAPTER 19
OUR PARENTS WON'T FEED US!

The small SUV was loaded with a portable generator, two movie projectors, public-address system and all the tools for an outdoor show. This was the weekend that Paul was invited to Marko's village to show the Jesus film. The powerful movie titled Jesus was a very convincing tool that helped the people of Guinea to understand the Gospel story.

Marko was a senior at the Bible School. He looked forward to the day when he would be sent to a remote village in the Guinea forest. There he would live and teach the Gospel of Jesus. He often wondered how all of his people of Guinea would ever hear about Jesus.

Paul and Marko squeezed into the 4 x 4. They prayed for God's protection as they traveled to the remote village.

They drove on Route 1 for some miles, and then they turned onto a trail in the tall elephant grass and followed two-wheel tracks. It had rained earlier in the week leaving a soggy road. Paul avoided large rocks and deep holes as the car crawled forward in four-wheel-drive.

As they entered a thick forest area, Paul tried to steer the wheels high above two deep ruts, but they slid in and were stuck. The ruts, like ditches, were deeper than the wheels, so the tires couldn't get any traction.

How do you get a 4 x 4 unstuck when the wheels aren't touching the ground? Tires turning on air don't get traction!

Paul pointed ahead to a large jungle tree. "Marko, let's clear the brush from that tree. We'll tie the cable there."

While Marko hacked around the base of the tree with a machete, Paul unwrapped the winch cable and extended it to the tree trunk where he attached it.

"Marko, move away from the cable in case it breaks loose." Paul warned.

Paul engaged the winch, and it slowly wound the cable. As it tightened around the spool, the vehicle began to drag itself out of the hole until all the wheels were back on the ground.

"Thank you, Jesus!" exclaimed Marko.

A large crowd lined the roadway as they drove into Marko's village. People sang and danced to greet them. They parked beside the chapel and a church elder opened their car doors to help them out. Everyone shook hands and gave them greetings. As they sat down in the pastor's home, cola nuts were passed around, and water was given to everyone to welcome them.

"Pastor Paul...," began Pastor Luke, "welcome to our home and to our village. Our home is your home. We have waited for a long time to greet you. Many people are coming from all around to see Jesus tonight. We have prayed much for this day."

Paul received his welcome, tasted a cola nut, drank the water, and they began to talk about their families.

At sunset, two church elders took a large white bed sheet and suspended it ten feet in the air on two bamboo poles. The movie screen was in place.

Paul and Marko set up the two movie projectors that would provide a continuous visual during four reels and two hours of movie. The small generator was placed away from the crowd where the noise and exhaust would not hinder the show.

As the evening star appeared in the sky, and the sun had set, people began to arrive. They came with mats and chairs. Children came with chunks of firewood to sit on. When it was dark, several hundred people were waiting in the square.

The choir led the people in worship. Paul preached a short message about the proof that Jesus is the Son of God. The pastor introduced the movie and the projector began to roll.

While the pastor explained the movie scenes to people who had never heard the Story, Paul sat back in his chair and relaxed. He looked up to a perfectly dark sky where millions of stars shone down on them like theater lights.

106

"Thank you, Jesus…," he prayed, "that Your Story can be told in such an awesome theater." He prayed that the powerful Name of Jesus would protect the projector and electronics from harm.

Missionaries and pastors had observed a peculiar glitch. Often, just as the film came to the crucifixion of Jesus, or the resurrection, a fuse burned out, or a light bulb popped, or something would happen to the generator. The Enemy knew how to stop the Story at the most important place so that the people would not see it. He wanted to keep God from visiting the people.

Thankfully, on this night the projectors and movies rolled without incident. As the crowd watched Jesus being crucified, they were completely silent. They wondered why this had happened to such a perfect Teacher. Then, as Mary entered the tomb on Easter Sunday, and saw the living Christ, the African crowd broke into wild cheering and yelling. The people understood the victory of Jesus over death. They saw it!

After the film, the pastor invited people to make a decision. A large number of young adults came to pray. Some Muslim teens came to Marko with a question. "Is that story true?"

"Yes, just like you read it in the Injil [the Gospels]," Marko answered.

"We want to believe this…," they continued, "…but if we follow Jesus tonight, our parents will not feed us tomorrow." They spoke of the terrible persecution they would experience if they followed Jesus.

They understood Jesus' words, *"If anyone would become My disciple, he must deny himself and take up his cross daily and follow Me"* (Luke 9:23).

The young men walked away sad. They knew now that Jesus is the Son of God, but their family set the rules: the cost of following Jesus was too great.

THOUGHT QUESTIONS:
CHAPTER 19
OUR PARENTS WON'T FEED US!

There are many people in the world who know that Jesus is God's Son, and that He will forgive them and accept them into His family. But they cannot make the decision to follow Jesus because they are afraid of what will happen to them if they choose Him instead of the religion of their family.

1.   Read Luke 9:23-27—In what different ways does Jesus describe the meaning of following Him? Memorize Luke 9:23.

2.   The boys learned that Jesus is really the Son of God, and they wanted to follow Him. Why was it impossible for them to follow Jesus at their age?

3.   What are some things that keep you from following Jesus? How can you overcome those things?

CHAPTER 20
BANDITS ATTACK!

The war in Liberia and Sierra Leon was spilling over into Guinea. In spite of all the efforts to contain the fighting, rebels came across the border through the unprotected jungles and waterways. Conakry had become a city of 500,000 people who never knew if they would sleep through a night without bandits breaking in.

How does one set his mind at peace during war?

Paul had driven to Conakry for three days of board meetings. He and Al, the Team Leader, came home after the second full day of sitting on hard benches. They were hoping for a quiet night. Al's house was protected inside a walled compound. In his house was the metal safety deposit box in which all of the money for salaries and projects was stored. In Conakry, people assumed that large sums of money are safer in someone's home than in an office building.

After dinner and a time to write letters and read, everyone went to bed and quickly fell asleep.

Suddenly, at 3:00 a.m., there were clicking guns outside.

Al went to his window and called out, "Who is there?"

More guns clicked and a voice spoke in heavily accented English, "Give us money or we shoot!"

Al ran to the living room and turned on the lights. It helped everyone inside to see where they were walking, but it also helped the bandits outside to see people in the house. And they had the guns!

Al looked across the living room at the boys' room where Paul stood. "Get the baseball bats in there!" he ordered pointing to the closet.

They both leaped into the boys' room diving for the closet. They each grabbed a bat: Al got the wood bat and Paul was stuck with the plastic bat!

"A lot of help this is!" Paul grumbled.

The bandits were shaking the steel front door trying to break the three bolt locks. They put a crowbar into a crack and jerked it to break the seal. There was a machine gun burst, and a bullet flew across the room lodging in the kitchen doorframe—eighteen inches above Carol's head, Al's wife.

All three now realized that if the bandits broke the door, they could be killed. Knowing that the thieves understood English, the three missionaries begin to plead with God in loud voices.

"Jesus, in your Name, strike these people with fear. Bring down your anger upon them," one pled.

"In Jesus' Name bind their evil desires! Protect us, Lord." They prayed in this way for several minutes, all the while watching the front steel door that was becoming more and more unstable.

Suddenly, all was quiet. The silence was as frightening as when the bandits were yelling. But what were they doing in silence? Were they about to burst into the room and slaughter them?

Carol looked at Al, "Maybe they're gone!"

Al turned out the lights and peered into the dark. He didn't see anyone.

Suddenly, the police appeared with submachine guns. Their captain gave orders to his men to cover the whole compound, and told the missionaries to stay inside. About five minutes later two men came to the front porch and asked them to come out.

They pushed forward the night guard of the compound and asked Al, "Do you recognize him?"

"Yes, he's our night guard," Al said, then pointing at the shaking dog he commented, "...and he's Walter, our watch dog, ...but he didn't watch very well tonight!"

They laughed at the poor shivering dog and the tension was broken.

The police wrote their report and then left. Everyone went back to bed, but nobody slept. There had been far too much anxiety for one night.

Why did the bandits give up and leave?

Perhaps they heard the police. Perhaps the prayers frightened them.

One thing the missionaries knew, *"The Lord will keep you from all harm—he will watch over your life"* (Psalm 121:7). He had done just that.

THOUGHT QUESTIONS:
CHAPTER 20
BANDITS ATTACK!

Nobody wants to be attacked by bandits, even when they know God's promise of protection, but it can still happen! When we understand this, we must learn to trust God to watch over us. He promises to protect us and to guide us even when we are not in a safe place.

1.   Read Psalm 91:1-5—What does God promise to those who fully trust Him? Memorize Psalm 121:7-8.

2.   What did God do this night that showed Paul and the others   that not even "the terror at night" would harm them?

3.   What should you do when you are in a terrifying experience?

CHAPTER 21
NOT REALLY CHRISTIANS

"Beep, Beep."

The pick-up truck's horn was calling to the students. Every Saturday, a teacher from the Bible School took a truckload of students to market where they would sell their garden products and purchase food items for the week.

As Paul drove the truck into town to the market, the students were singing. Twenty-five voices in the back of the pickup harmonized in a joyful noise, announcing their arrival.

Paul walked around the market greeting merchant friends. Each seller had his cubbyhole where he stored and sold his wares. As Paul walked along the narrow hall between the stores, salesmen who knew him would call out.

"Hey, Pastor, how are you this week? I haven't seen you for many days," one man said.

Paul stopped and shook hands with an elderly gentleman. His long white beard sat on his chest. "That clock you sold me really works well!" Paul announced.

"Oh sure, sure. You know I only sell things guaranteed from China. All good! All good!" and he patted his chest with pride.

"Hey pastor, come…I have a question." another merchant called out to him.

Paul stepped over to the Coca Cola man's stall. The vendor sold soft drinks by the case, or by the truckload.

"Greetings," Paul said, shaking his hand. "How are your wives and children?"

"All is good, all is good." the man announced cheerfully. "How is your wife?" he inquired, seeing Marian near Paul.

"My one wife is very happy." Paul declared emphasizing the number one.

"Only one wife!" he exclaimed. "You should have at least five wives!" he declared, being sure to keep the number to the Prophet's quota of five wives for one man.[5]

"Yes," Paul affirmed. "I have only one wife."

The wise men sitting on a bench began to stroke their white beards.

"Now, you know your Koran," Paul began, "How many wives did God give to Adam?" he asked.

"Only one," they all agreed.

"So, if God knew that Adam could only manage one wife, and He said she was 'good,' why do you think that you should have five?"

The old men stroked their beards faster, as they mumbled in agreement.

Paul continued as he looked from one man to the other sitting on the bench. "Listen, I have only one wife in my house and there is always peace."

"You have a point there!" they all agreed. "Our house has no peace because we have too many wives."

Paul shook hands all around and continued his shopping.

He walked by the fabric store. The man inside, a Muslim missionary and store manager, called to him, "Pastor, come in. Drink some tea." He handed Paul a fresh cup of chai—a very strong African tea. He showed the deep friendship he felt for Paul.

"Thank you," Paul said, as he sat down.

---

[5] The Prophet Mohammed instructs in the Koran that one man should limit himself to no more than five wives.

Paul saw a book on the table. He picked it up, and as he paged through it, he saw it was a storybook from a leading false cult that was illegally entering into Guinea. The cult was trying to influence this man.

Paul turned the pages, then looked up and asked the Imam[6], "My friend, did you read this book?"

"Yes," he responded.

Paul continued, "Did you see that these are pictures of what they believe heaven is like?"

"Yes."

Paul added, "Did you notice that there are no black faces in their paradise?"

He came over to look, still sipping his tea. "You are right. I never thought of that. They don't think black people will be in their heaven!"

He paused to think, then asked again, "Pastor, this group is not really Christian, is it?"

Paul was surprised at his perceptiveness. "No, they are not Christian even if they say they are. What made you suspicious?"

"Because, even though they talk about Jesus, they do not believe that He is the Son of God," he remarked.

"That is exactly right," affirmed Paul, "and that is the real difference!"

They talked more about the subject until the tea was gone. Paul was amazed that this Muslim missionary was able to discern the lie of a false religion that claims to be Christian. He understood the words, *"No one who denies the Son has the Father; whoever acknowledges the Son has the Father"* (1 John 2:23).

---

[6] The Imam is the priest who leads the Mosque.

THOUGHT QUESTIONS:
CHAPTER 21
NOT REALLY CHRISTIAN

The Imam was a very religious man and a missionary sent from Mali to teach the Muslim religion to the people of Kissidougou. He and Paul became friends, which made it possible for them to talk about their different beliefs. Paul was surprised on the day that the Imam talked about a false religion that came to Guinea, because the Imam described the difference between a true "Christian" and this false group.

1.   Read 2 Timothy 4:1-5—What do these verses describe as the proofs that a person is really a follower of Jesus, a "true Christian"? Memorize 1 John 2:23.

2.   What did this Imam, who is not a Christian, reveal about a false religion that told him that their belief was also not Christian?

3.   Who are there around you that say they are Christians but really aren't? In what ways can you show them God's love—like 2 Timothy 4:1-5 describes—without arguing with them?

CHAPTER 22
NO CHRISTIANS THERE!

"Ko Ko Ko!" Pastor John was at the door.

"Come in, Pastor." Paul had been expecting him for several days. Pastor John came from a remote village on the border with Sierra Leone.

He sat down and drank a glass of water before he began.

"Pastor Paul, I need you to come to my village of Bolodou to teach the Gospel. It has been many months now that people are asking to see the Jesus Story."

Together, they chose a date.

On the designated Friday, Paul left Telekoro with a student, Samuel, for Bolodou. They found Pastor John waiting for them at the path that turned off Route 1.

As John rode with them he explained, "This road is very difficult. Many people get lost because there are places where there is no road."

Paul wondered what this meant? However, with 4 x 4 and a winch up front, he was confident that they could make their way. An African proverb says, "Where there is a voice, you won't lose the road." It means that so long as there is someone to show the way, you won't get lost.

They crawled forward through the jungle, and then on a prairie trail, for two hours. Finally, they drove through a stream and climbed the bank. As they drove up to the pastor's chapel and house, Paul looked at the odometer and saw that it had taken them two hours to drive 14 miles.

"That was some road!" Paul exclaimed to John.

Paul settled into his small room fitted with a table, chair and a small, stuffed mattress bed. He prayed that the Holy Spirit would fill this weekend with His presence and power.

John's wife invited them to a dinner of rice and goat sauce with greens. As they ate the hearty meal, Paul asked, "Tell me why you came to this village that is so far away."

Pastor John said, "My wife and I were at a very nice large city church. We were comfortable, and many people were coming to Jesus. But, as the years passed, the Spirit showed us that we were supposed to leave our comfort and go plant a church where there were no Jesus followers. In time, we heard about this village. We were told that it was a village with some Muslim followers and mostly ancestor worshippers…but no Christians. After much prayer, we were convinced that the Holy Spirit was sending us here.

"So, we went to the church leaders and asked that they send us here.

"'Why do you want to go there?' they asked. 'No Christians live there, and there is no way we can support you there!'

"They were very fearful that we would die of starvation or for other reasons.

"We told them that God was sending us to a place where there were no Christians!

"So, they let us go and said that they would pray for us.

"We packed our belongings and came here, not knowing anyone or where we would get food. We only knew that the Holy Spirit wanted us to come. When we arrived, we went to visit the Chieftain and Elders. We asked them for a piece of land to plant a garden and a place to build a worship house. They knew we were Christians, and they refused to provide what we asked of them. So, we blessed them and came out of the village.

"We sat down right across the path from here and began to pray that God would show us where we could begin. When we had prayed, we looked up and saw this piece of property. Tall eucalyptus trees surrounded it, but it was full of weeds and trash.

"Just then, some villagers walked by. We asked them, 'Why is this land empty?'

"They nervously told us that the land is inhabited by demons and nobody can use it!

"In that moment, my wife and I knew where we would live! We prayed for this land, and then walked back to see the Chief. We asked him about this piece and he said the same thing, 'It is possessed by demons. No one can live there or plant anything there.'

"We asked to live there.

"He called the Elders together, and they gladly gave us the land, since it was so useless to them.

"We came back rejoicing that God had given us land and that it was right along the main path to the village. We walked around the parcel three times claiming the land in the Name of Jesus and ordering the demons to return to hell! We prayed for the Blood of Jesus to cleanse it from all evil and impurity. When we knew they had gone, we brought our baggage and moved in.

"Today, everyone knows that the power of the Name of Jesus is greater than their demon spirits, and the Christians know the God who chases evil away. This place truly belongs to Jesus!" he concluded victoriously.

That evening, John told Paul of the many ways that God was opening doors to peoples' hearts. He depended only on prayer and Jesus to protect them and lead them.

Paul asked, "But, I haven't heard the call to prayer yet." It was unusual to not hear the sundown call.

"Oh, that's another answer to prayer!" John exclaimed. "When I came, I noticed that the Imam would call people to pray in his small mosque. But I also saw that there were not many who believed. I began to pray that the Holy Spirit would make him so unhappy here that he would leave. I prayed for him and talked to him about Jesus for five years. One day, as I came to the village square, I saw him on his bike packed for travel. I asked what he was doing.

"He said, 'I'm leaving. People don't want faith in Allah here!'

"I wished him a good trip. No one has called for prayer to Allah from that day to this," John concluded.

Paul went to his bed that evening marveling at the power of God to protect. Through Pastor John's obedience, God was claiming this village for Himself. John and his wife lived the words of Jesus, *"If you believe, you will receive whatever you ask for in prayer"* (Matthew 21:22).

What would he meet tomorrow?

THOUGHT QUESTIONS:
CHAPTER 22
NO CHRISTIANS THERE!

The Holy Spirit sends some people to tell others about Jesus who have never heard, and may not want to hear about Him. This story and the following two stories describe the challenge of taking the Gospel to very difficult people groups.

Paul and Marian learned through these events that even though we don't understand everything about praying to God in Jesus' Name, we know that He hears and answers in His way.

1.   Read Matthew 21:18-22—What lesson did Jesus teach about the importance of prayer? Memorize Matthew 21:22.

2.   What did Pastor John do even though many Christians said that they shouldn't go to this village?

3.   Why is it important that you obey the Holy Spirit when he tells you to do something even though some people don't think you should do it?

4.   How can the habit of praying to God and talking with Him be important and helpful to your Christian life?

CHAPTER 23
TREMBLING KNEES

People were streaming past the church property on their way to the market. As Paul and Samuel finished breakfast, Pastor John invited them to go into the village.

"It is the custom that the special guest meets the village Chieftain. This is a good time for us to go find him." John explained.

They exited the churchyard and walked slowly up the hill to the center of the village. Paul looked back at the property that had been rescued from demons and was now a lighthouse for Jesus. He wondered what God would do on this day?

As they walked, Pastor John explained, "I need to tell you about the Chief. He is the most powerful sorcerer in the region."

"You mean like a witch doctor or shaman?"[7] asked Paul.

"Yes," continued John. "He specializes in long distance curses. If a person wants to take vengeance on his enemy, he will come to this village and pay a price of a goat or a chicken. The shaman will sacrifice the animal on an altar in his sacred forest. He will order his demons to go to the village of the named enemy. The spirits will kill that person within ten days."

Paul was curious. He had heard of these kinds of things, but this sounded pretty powerful. "How effective is he?" he asked John.

"He makes his living doing this. Important political people drive over that terrible road to this village and pay him to make vengeance. It works because people keep coming back to him."

---

[7] The footnote on page 46 explains the role of the witchdoctor.

Paul realized that this man was powerful in the Kingdom of Darkness. He wondered what this day would end like if they were going to declare the Name of Jesus to this man's people.

They arrived in the center of the village. Pastor John took Paul and Samuel to an elderly man sitting on a boulder beside the square. As they approached, John introduced him to Paul. They exchanged greetings, and the pastor gave him the traditional cola nuts. The Chieftain assured Paul that he was pleased to have them speak the Words of God in his front yard—the town square.

Paul thanked him for his reception. Then John said to the Chieftain, "Please, come with us to the school principal's house. Pastor Paul has a message for you."

That was a surprise to Paul! Paul wondered what he was going to say? This wasn't a planned speech, but obviously the Pastor expected Paul to share the Gospel with the Chieftain.

As they walked, Paul began to pray for the Spirit to tell him what to say, "Jesus give me your thoughts...fast!"

They entered the Principal's house and sat down in the lounge. The pastor was to one side of Paul facing the Chief. After greeting their host, Pastor John repeated his statement, "Mr. Chief, Pastor Paul would like to say something to you."

Paul prayed and wondered what he was going to say, 'Holy Spirit, give me the words now!'"

He again greeted the Chief, and then said, "I'm a stranger in your village. I am much younger than you and lack the experience of life that you have. I cannot speak except that you first tell me your words as my elder."

After a silence, the Chief began to talk. "I have always been a good man and open to other religions, especially to Christians. My second wife is a Christian. And the Principal used to be my enemy until he found Jesus then he was totally changed and now we are friends. I welcome you to my village to tell us your news." He stopped.

It was time for Paul to speak. "I am honored to be in your presence this weekend. Thank you for receiving us. I have lived in Africa for many years. The ancients often said, 'Look, Listen, and Understand, then make a decision.' The village elders always make their decisions this way. Is that how you do it here?"

The chief shook his head, "Yes, always."

Paul continued, "You told me that your wife is a Christian. You said that this Principal completely changed when he found Jesus. So, you have seen what Jesus does.

"Pastor John has spoken to you many times about Jesus, so you have heard what Jesus can do.

"You are a great man of deep understanding—you would not be the village Chief if you did not have understanding. So, I know that you understand what Jesus can do for you."

Paul came to the important question.

"When will you decide to follow Jesus?"

There was a long pause that was finally broken by Samuel, the student. He was frustrated, "Well aren't you going to give the Pastor an answer?" Samuel should not have spoken, but now the words were out.

The Chief looked at Samuel with disgust. He stood up facing Samuel, and brushed the dust off of his robes as if to wipe away the truth. Then he said to Samuel, "You are too young to understand what we talked about this morning."

He turned and walked out of the room without another word. This was ominous!

That evening the people gathered in the Chief's courtyard. The Chieftain was sitting in the front row. More than 300 people had come from the nearby villages. They listened to the small group of Christians from Pastor John's chapel sing and share some words of testimony. Paul preached a short message about being transformed by Jesus.

Pastor John stood in the center of the square and made a brief invitation, "You have heard that Jesus, The Resurrected One, changes hearts. If you want Him to transform your life, come and kneel here with me."

He waited a minute, then people started coming forward. Soon seventy people, mostly young adults, were kneeling around him and asking Jesus to forgive them and change their hearts.

But the Chief sat and watched. In his mind, he saw seventy people leave his Kingdom of Darkness and go into the Kingdom of Jesus. These young people would no longer be under his powerful magic spells.

He lost seventy souls this night! And he knew it!

The movie began to roll and the crowd settled in to watch. Pastor John explained and translated every word and scene. When the crowd saw Jesus arrested, Pastor John explained how the events showed Jesus as King.

As Jesus stood before Pilate, Herod and the Sanhedrin, the Chieftain became agitated. His legs were shaking, and he asked Pastor John to come and sit next to him. He asked the pastor, "Why are those people treating Jesus this way? Jesus is innocent!"

John answered into the microphone so that the crowd heard his response.

As the soldiers whipped Jesus, the Chief was shaking with frustration, and he cried out, "This is unfair!"

John continued to share the Chief's questions over the microphone. Everyone became silent as Jesus was lifted up on the cross, and again, as He was taken down and laid in the tomb.

Soon the night had passed, and Easter morning dawned. Mary entered the tomb. When she saw Jesus sitting on the rock table, the African crowd cheered ecstatically. They saw that the Man who overcame death is the Man who changes people today!

The Chieftain had heard and seen the Truth again. He understood even more clearly that Jesus died for his sins. But he couldn't decide to follow Jesus, even though he knew Jesus said, *"I am the way and the truth and the life. No one comes to the Father except through Me"* (John 14:6).

Everyone returned to their houses wondering about this Jesus who visited them that night.

The Chieftain went to bed pondering his next move.

THOUGHT QUESTIONS:
CHAPTER 23
TREMBLING KNEES

The village Chieftain was a very powerful man in the world of evil, but on this night, he saw the power of Jesus. He learned things about Jesus' story that he had not understood before. This revealed to him why his power over people was slowly dwindling. When the day ended, he knew that Jesus is alive and very powerful—stronger than his chieftainship.

1.   Read John 14:1-6—What are the different reasons Jesus gives us so that we are not troubled.? Memorize John 14:6.

2.   Why did the chieftain tremble that night? What are all the things he heard and saw that made him afraid?

3.   Describe the time that you decided to trust Jesus as the only way to the Father? What changed in your life after that?

CHAPTER 24
THROUGH THE FIRE!

"Paul," Marian said at breakfast, "we have guests coming to stay in the apartment, but the stove doesn't work. Could you and Dave check to see if it's all right, and connect it to a propane tank?"

"Sure," Paul agreed, adding this to a long to do list of the day.

David, his neighbor, came to help with the campus chores, and they went to the stove that needed repair.

"Fixing this will be a piece of cake," David said, as he examined the stove. "It just needs a copper tube adapter on the back so the gas hose will connect safely."

They found the material needed, and carried the stove to the back porch where they were going to repair it. Paul charged a Coleman kerosene torch that would be used to solder the tube to the stove. As he pumped up the pressure, Nathan was sitting nearby on the steps and watching them work.

David saw a yellow flame coming out of the torch. "Paul," he warned, "that flame should be blue. Are you sure the torch is all right?"

"I think so," responded Paul. "The repairman brought it back earlier this week, and it worked O.K."

Paul saw that the pressure wasn't holding in the torch. "Perhaps there's an air leak?"

He began to adjust the pressure release valve when suddenly it came unscrewed and blew flaming fuel onto Paul's chest and legs. The power of the explosion was so strong that it threw Paul three feet backward against the brick wall of his house. His left elbow hit the wall breaking the force of his fall.

Paul saw flames on his shirt and pants and quickly ran to the driveway.

Nathan jumped out of the way as his Dad flew over the steps onto the ground, rolling in the dirt to put out the flames. His shirt had been reduced to black char, and his left pant leg was burned to ashes.

Paul jumped to his feet and moved towards the water faucet, his skin burning-hot, and he fell to the ground again. David grabbed the hose and sprayed water over his burned chest and legs.

Amadou, a senior student from the college, was walking by and saw Paul lying on the ground, and his chest and pants all burned. He was horrified, and he turned away praying, "Jesus, save my professor."

Laura, David's wife, quickly came to Paul. She was trained in physical therapy and burn treatment. She saw that Paul's shoulder was dislocated and in an unnatural position. Laura helped Paul stand up and guided his steps into a room where Marian had quickly made up a bed. As he lay down on the bed, his body went into shock, shaking uncontrollably. Paul felt excruciating pain from his chest to his legs and shoulder. It felt like he was still on fire!

Meanwhile, David ran for the car and rushed into Kissidougou to call the German doctor.

The doctor, having just flown in from the coast, grabbed her bag and went with David, arriving thirty minutes later. She gave Paul a shot of morphine, which calmed his shaking, but didn't reduce the pain. As the doctor surveyed the burns, she estimated that 10-15% of his body was burned with second- and third-degree burns.

With the help of Diane, the school nurse, they put burn-gauze on his body.

A women's group in an American church had given special burn wound pads to Diane for the school pharmacy, which had been on the shelf for many years. Now they were well beyond their usable date. Diane had thought about throwing them away, but didn't because there wasn't a hospital emergency room, and her supplies were limited. Now, she had exactly what Paul needed, even though outdated.

Once the doctor and Diane had covered the wounds, they wrapped so many bandages around Paul's chest and legs that he looked like a mummy. However, his left shoulder was still out of its socket. After trying to reset it, the doctor decided to go into the small hospital where she hoped the X-ray unit might be working. She hoped it would show them the best way to manipulate Paul's shoulder into its proper position.

Paul came into the X-ray room. There was only a wooden table to lie on. The technician, who happened to be working this day, placed the X-ray machine over Paul's shoulder and clicked the switch. He took the negative into the lab. Fortunately, he had chemicals on hand to develop the image this day. This wasn't always the case.

Looking at the X-ray, the doctor, with the help of others, tried to reset Paul's shoulder, but it would not go in. It had been more than two hours since the accident, and his muscles had tightened.

After putting Paul to sleep with a mild anesthesia, they forced the shoulder back in place. Even under anesthesia, Paul remembered yelling in pain as his shoulder and socket reconnected. After that, the pain of his dislocated shoulder began to dissipate.

That night, as Paul and Marian talked about the day, they realized that God had known well in advance that this would be a day when he would again come very close to death—the second time in his life.

His accident had happened where there was little medical care. However, the right people, the right supplies and the right equipment were present and functioning when needed. God had saved him again!

On that same day, communications with the capital city, and from Guinea to the United States, were operational. That was not always possible. Within ten hours Christians in churches across America were praying for Paul's healing.

As Paul tried to sleep that night he thought about the prophet's words, *"When you walk through the fire you will not be burned; the flames will not set you ablaze"* (Isaiah 43:2b).

Although Paul and David wondered later why the accident had happened, it became apparent to them that the Lord had stepped into Africa again to intervene for a life!

THOUGHT QUESTIONS:
CHAPTER 24
THROUGH THE FIRE!

Ten days after the conversation with the Chieftain, Pastor Paul was burned in a blowtorch accident. From a human point of view, this was an accident caused by a defective machine. It happened in a place in Africa where medical help is very poor, especially for serious burns. Paul again was in danger of death, yet God kept His promise to protect and heal.

1.   Read Isaiah 43:1-5—What does God promise to those who fully trust Him? Memorize Isaiah 43:2-3a.

2.   Make a list of the different ways God intervened in this emergency. One example: the only local doctor had just arrived from out of town when David called her.

3.   The promise in Isaiah 43 is about God's intervention on behalf of those whom He calls. Think about different events in your life. What are ways that God has protected you from evil and danger?

CHAPTER 25
I'M STILL ALIVE!

No mosquito would touch him! They buzzed at a safe distance!

Paul was in bed swallowing double portions of antibiotic—so much of it that he smelled like penicillin! This was one advantage to his pain—no mosquito bites.

The gardener came in to visit him. He saw Paul wrapped like a mummy, and he began to wail and weep as though Paul were dying. It is customary that when visiting the ill person, you must show that you feel his pain, so he wailed.

"Moses! Moses!" Paul called out. "Please pray that I will be healed."

Moses stopped wailing, wiped away his tears, and he began to plead with Jesus to touch the burns.

Students and pastors came to visit. They prayed for Paul. People in America and around the world were praying for him.

One morning, after the bandages were changed, David came to visit. "I've been thinking about the accident. It seemed so strange," he observed.

Paul responded, "Me, too."

David continued, "I have been studying this from a mechanical perspective. I took the torch apart and put it back together again. Then, I got it burning and tried to make it do what it did to you, and it would not repeat that action!" He said this with incredulity.

Paul thought for a moment, "That matches what I've been thinking. Perhaps I triggered the accident in some way, but you say it could not happen a second time?"

"That's why this is strange," David affirmed.

Paul said, "I've been reading Job's story. Job didn't ask for the illness, but God allowed Satan to bring misery to his life to prove to Satan that his power is no match for God."

"Hmm, that's interesting," David mused.

Paul continued the thought, "Is there someone that God needs to demonstrate His glory to, someone who would have a connection to me?" he asked.

David asked, "What about that witch doctor you talked to?"

Paul suddenly had an idea. "That accident happened exactly ten days after I shared the Gospel with him. He guarantees that his demons will get you in ten days!" he exclaimed.

"You know what?" David added. "We should think more about this. Maybe it was more than a mechanical accident. Maybe that man needs to know that he does not have power against Jesus' Name."

They prayed together, and David left to teach his class.

Every day Diane and Laura took off his bandages, removing dead skin, and cleaned his wounds so that new skin could grow.

On the seventh day, Paul sat up for the daily routine. They undid his mummy wrap, and all of the burn pads fell off his body. He had new skin—pink like a baby—all over his chest, stomach, and leg. In seven days, God had answered the prayers of people around the world. He completely replaced the old skin.

Two months later, Pastor John came to visit Paul. He talked about the wonderful new group of believers at the church. The congregation had doubled in number. He thanked Paul for coming to share the Gospel.

After praying with Paul, he got up to leave and Paul asked a question, "Pastor John, does the Chieftain ask about my health?"

John looked perplexed and answered, "Yes, he does ask from time to time."

Paul began, "Next time he asks would you please say to him, 'Pastor Paul is doing well; he is still alive!'"

Pastor John protested, "But Satan can't touch you! Why should I tell him that?"

"It's true, Satan can't touch me, if God wills. But remember? God used pain in Job's life to show Satan that he has no power."

"You are right, Pastor." He turned to walk away, deep in thought, and then turned about and said "Good-by, Pastor."

"Good-bye, and safe travel." Paul wished him the best.

After Paul's healing, he often reflected on Job's conviction. *"Though He [God] slay me, yet will I hope in Him"* (Job 13:15). *"I know that my Redeemer lives, and that in the end He will stand upon the earth; ..."* (Job 19:25). God is much more powerful than anything people might hope for. When the earth itself ends, He will stand.

THOUGHT QUESTIONS:
CHAPTER 25
I'M STILL ALIVE!

As the days passed, Paul's burns healed. He meditated on God's Word and reviewed all of the events. David, his neighbor, was also thinking about this. One day as they talked, pieces of the puzzle came together and they began to understand why this accident happened. Serving our powerful God means allowing Him to use us as an instrument of Truth-telling to those who have never heard. Being God's instrument is sometimes costly.

1. Read Job 13:15, 19:25—Why could Job have complete confidence in God? Memorize Job 19:25.

2. What lesson do you think God wanted to teach the Chieftain?

3. What truth in this story helps you to still trust God, even if it is a tough time?

CHAPTER 26
GOD IS THERE!

It was an old, moldy school bus called "Rapido".

But the bus had lost all of its "Rapido". Now, it cost more money to fix than to drive, so the school board asked Paul to sell it.

Word spread by the grape vine around Kissidougou that the college was selling the Rapido. Merchants began to dream of the money they would make by filling the 15-passenger bus with 40 people at one time! As visions of money danced in their heads the bus sat rusting.

Then, a chauffeur-driven sedan pulled up to Paul's office. A seventy-year-old gentleman in flowing Muslim robes stepped out of the car and greeted Paul.

"Greetings, sir," he began with respect, and tapped his hand to his chest as a sign of wishing the blessings of Allah for Paul.

"Greetings, sir." Paul responded. "How is the family?"

"They are good...and you?" he countered.

"They are good...and your wives and children?" Paul continued.

"May Allah be blessed...they are good." he responded, asking Paul the same question.

Once the greetings were completed, he came to the subject, "I heard that you are selling a Rapido?"

"Oh, yes!" said Paul, wondering why anyone would want the old beast. "Would you like to come with me to see it?"

"Yes!" The man's chauffeur joined them as they walked to the rusty bus, looking very dirty, moldy and dead. He walked around it, commenting to his driver that it was so beautiful.

As he moved around the bus, Paul noticed that the elderly man was having so much trouble breathing that it was hard to walk. A mere pace of four steps took the man's wind away. Paul smelled cigarette smoke on the man's clothing. As he listened, he concluded that the man either had emphysema or lung cancer. Paul knew the symptoms because some of his family members had died of this illness.

The man looked at Paul. Between deep gasps for air, he said, "It's the most beautiful thing I have ever seen. Let's talk about the price."

"Of course," responded Paul, "let's go into my home where it is cool."

They walked slowly to the house, and entered the sitting room to escape the tropical heat.

Once seated, they agreed to a price.

"I will bring the first payment to you in one week," promised the man as he gasped for air.

They shook hands, and then Paul observed, "I see that you struggle to breath. It must be very painful."

"Oh, sir...," he began his story, "this problem began two years ago. I am a man of money, and so I traveled to Sierra Leone and other countries to find a doctor who could help me. But they only prescribed more medications. Nothing has helped, and my breathing gets worse," he concluded with a gasping sigh.

Paul knew that Mamadou believed there is a god. However, Paul also knew that Mamadou's god is not there—and that he doesn't care.

Paul walked with Mamadou to the car. Once he was seated and waiting, Paul asked, "Would you let me pray for your illness in Jesus' Name?"

The Koran requires the devout Muslim to respect Jews and Christians as "the people of prayer." As a result, they must obey their Koran when a Christian prays, just as a Christian shows respect to them during their five daily prayers.

Before he could refuse, Paul said, "Let's pray!" and he began.

"Father in heaven, I thank You for being a God who is all powerful and who hears us when we pray. I thank You that Issa [Arabic for Jesus] came to forgive us, and to deliver us from our sin. I thank You that He died on the cross so that all who trust Him will be forgiven. Thank You that Issa rose again from death to have victory over our illness. So, Lord Jesus, I place my friend, Mamadou, into Your hand, and I ask that by the power of the Name of Issa, and by His death and resurrection, please touch his breathing so that he knows, without any doubt, that You did it. May he rest easier knowing that the Messiah heard and answered our prayer. Amina."

Mr. Mamadou stared ahead without blinking during the prayer, and when Paul concluded, he respectfully repeated, "Amina."

The chauffeur stepped on the accelerator and they drove away.

Paul wondered what would come from this encounter.

Seven days later the man returned. The chauffeur stopped in the same spot. Paul and the old man shared the same greeting. They went into the house and sat down on the same chairs. Mamadou was still breathing hard, but with less visible stress.

"There it is…," he declared, "all of it!" as he put a big sack of money on the coffee table.

Paul counted the money. They signed the legal documents and the bus was his. Paul was happy this story had ended, and thought the man would want to be on his way with his Rapido.

As Paul stood up to escort Mamadou out, the man reached out and grabbed Paul's arm.

"No!" he announced loudly and tugging Paul's arm. "I'm not leaving your house until you pray for me again in Issa's Name!"

Wow!

Paul wondered what brought this on!

He sat down, "What happened?" he asked.

Mamadou said, "I don't know what happened! I just know that it got better after you prayed in Issa's Name, so I won't leave till you do it again!"

Paul again prayed, this time giving thanks to God's for His mercy through Jesus' sacrifice. He again implored Jesus to touch the man and give him peace.

Mamadou was content.

Paul led him to his car, and they said goodbye.

Mr. Mamadou died of his illness two months later, but he died knowing that Issa, the Messiah, hears and answers prayers; and God gave peace to his lungs and his heart.

When Paul heard about his death, he sent a sack of rice as a gift of sorrow to the family.

Paul often meditated on the prayer of David, *"May God be gracious to us and bless us…that Your way mays be known on the earth, Your salvation among all nations"* (Psalm 67:1-2).

Mamadou died knowing Truth: "God IS there, and He does care!"

THOUGHT QUESTIONS:
CHAPTER 26
GOD IS THERE!

God has one desire for all people of every language-group in the world—that people from these groups would praise and worship Him. Paul shared the essential truth of the Gospel with the Muslim man who bought the school bus, and he understood.

1.   Read Psalm 67:1-7—How many times in these verses does he mention God's desire that the nations would hear about Him? Memorize Psalm 67:1-2.

2.   In what way did Mamadou hear and discover the power of God?

3.   How did Paul show he cared about the man, and how did he share the Gospel with him?

4.   In what ways can you share the Gospel with people that have never heard?

CHAPTER 27
BUT…MY FAMILY!

"Koko, Koko! Mr. Paul, are you here?" the man called.

Paul came to the door to greet the wood carver.

"Good morning. How are you today?" Paul asked as they shook hands.

"I am fine…and your wife?"

"She is doing well," Paul responded. "…and your wife and children?"

"God willing, yes!" he responded.

Paul wondered why he had come. "My friend, what event brings you here?"

"Oh, Mr. Paul," he began, "I want to show you my newest carving. You will want to buy it," he predicted as he pulled out a nicely carved elephant.

"That is very nice," Paul remarked. "Let's sit down and talk." He invited the man to sit on the steps.

After giving him a drink, they began.

"I have been here almost ten years…," Paul began, "and I have not bought carvings. You know that I've lived in Africa many years and I have a large collection of art."

"Oh yes," his visitor countered, "but these are not like anything you ever owned."

Paul wondered how he knew his collection didn't have these things. The man pulled another elephant out of the bag and began pressing a sale.

"These are very nice," agreed Paul, "but why is it you need to sell me something today?"

The salesman swallowed the rest of his water, and put down the glass, "My friend, tomorrow is the feast of Tabaski. All of my family waits for me to celebrate the sacrificial lamb with them."

"Oh," Paul understood. "Today you need to find the money to buy the lamb that you will sacrifice tomorrow?"

The Feast of Tabaski[5] in Guinea is essential for the Muslim. It commemorates the moment Abraham sacrificed Ishmael [not Isaac] on the altar. Every year the head of the household must purchase the sacrificial lamb, and as the oldest man cuts the sheep's throat, every male standing behind him places his hand on the shoulder of the one in front to receive the forgiveness coming from the blood of the sacrificed lamb. Then, the women cook the meat and they eat together rejoicing that, for another year, their sins are atoned—maybe. Without this event, a family would go through the next twelve months fearing that their souls are not right.

Paul continued, "You do this every year, don't you?"

"Yes, we do. It is important." he answered.

"What if it were discovered" Paul began, "that someone already made the perfect blood sacrifice that completely pleases God, and now through that One Sacrifice, we no longer need to make it? What would you do?" Paul was referring to the perfect sacrifice of Jesus described in the New Testament: *"We have been made holy through the sacrifice of the body of Jesus Christ once for all"* (Hebrews 10:10).

"Yes," the carver hesitated. He had heard about the sacrifice of Issa. He knew who Paul was talking about. "That would be wonderful," he agreed. He paused for a moment, then continued, "…but my family would not be happy. You know how that is!"

The Muslim man knew the truth about Jesus' sacrifice, yet he could not accept it because family pressure held him back.

---

[5] The annual Muslim feast of *Eid al-Adha* [some sects call it "Tabaski"] commemorates Abraham's sacrifice of son Ishmael on the altar. But Ishmael was preserved for life by the ram in the thicket. The Bible teaches that Isaac was put on the altar. See Genesis 22 and Koran, Sura 37:99-111 (Saffat).

"I'm sorry that it is so hard." Paul responded.

"Thank you for talking with me," the carver concluded, as he put his elephants back in the bag and wished him well.

THOUGHT QUESTIONS:
CHAPTER 27
BUT ... MY FAMILY!

The sacrifice of Jesus is different from any other religious sacrifice. Yet, many people in the world still believe that their kind of repeated sacrifice is the way that their sins will be forgiven. Sometimes they are so deeply tied to their kind of sacrifice that even when they hear about Jesus' death, they can't give up their way to follow Jesus.

1.   Read Hebrews 10:8-13—Why is the sacrifice of Jesus so different from sacrifices of all other religions? Memorize Hebrews 10:10.

2.   Why did the wood carver need to accept the sacrifice of Jesus in place of the annual sacrifice? Why couldn't he accept it?

3.   What are some ways that your family might keep you from fully following Jesus?

CHAPTER 28
COUNT THE COST OR BE LOST!

He had been the most powerful Imam (Muslim priest) in Sierra Leone. Amadou had been the Chief of his own mosque. To attain such high status, he had begun studying the Muslim holy book, the Koran, at age 5.

Pastor Paul wondered why this tall stately man had come from such power and status to study at the Bible School, so he invited Amadou for a conversation.

"Amadou, tell me," Paul began, "why did you leave the Muslim faith to become a Jesus follower?"

"I grew up in a Muslim family," He began. "We were very faithful to go to prayers every morning at 5:00. When I was five years old, I was sent to the Koranic school to learn the writings of Muhammed, the Prophet. I had my own writing tablet like that one you have." He pointed at the clean white board that was shaped like a thin tombstone.

Amadou took it and sat down low, "We sat on the floor like this." He placed his six-foot-two body on the rug and crossed his legs. In his lap he held the writing board. "We wrote with a stylus and a special washable ink on this board." He began to write the first chapter of the Koran on the tablet.

"It sounds like this." He began to chant with deep respect and in Arabic,

> *"In the name of God, most gracious, most merciful,*
> *Praise be to God, the Cherisher and Sustainer of the Worlds;*
> *Most Gracious, Most Merciful;*
> *Master of the Day of Judgment,*
> *Thee do we worship, And Thine aid we seek.*
> *Show us the straight way,*
> *The way of those on whom Thou hast bestowed thy Grace*
> *Those whose portion is not wrath, and who do not go astray."*
> [translated from the Koran Sura 1 (Fatiha)]

"Does everyone do that together?" Paul asked.

"Everyone. We have to memorize it perfectly because this is the primary prayer." Amadou answered.

"Do you have to repeat it in Arabic even if your mother language is Peuhlar?" asked Paul.

"Perfectly, in Arabic," he continued, "and by the end of two or three years, we learn the prayers and other principle verses, and some of the rules of Islam."

"What happens if you don't repeat it perfectly?" Paul asked.

Amadou sighed, "Then Allah does not accept our prayer."

"But…," Paul objected, "Arabic is not your native language! Is it true that people all over the world are praying five times a day in a language they don't understand, but they hope to say it right one time so Allah will accept them?"

"That is correct," he answered. "Sadly, most of the Muslim people in Africa do not understand what they say to their god."

Paul remembered that the God of Israel and Christians understands every language of every people group!

"Why did you decide to follow Jesus?" Paul asked.

"I learned the Koranic recitations perfectly so I could become an Imam. Then I took the blood vow over the dead body of one of the most powerful marabou[8] in Sierra Leone. With this vow, I gained the help of demons to do miracles."

He respectfully took a Koran on the desk.

---

[8] The Marabou is the Muslim religious leader who is also skilled in calling on occult and demonic powers to manipulate change in the body or a group of people. He also knows the secrets of herbs and trees. These powers are often associated with secret meanings of verses in the Koran.

Look here." He invited Paul to look at some verses.

"See that mark over the letter?" He pointed to a mark that looked like an Arabic accent. "That tells me that if you recite this verse 77 times before you come to a customs official at the border, he will not see you or your merchandise."

He pointed to other verses showing promises of healing, fertility for ladies, revenge on an enemy, and more.

He continued, "So, I had a very good income, I had a wife and two children. I had power and status in the community. I was a man of importance."

"Then what happened?" Paul wondered.

"Some students from a Christian school showed the Jesus film in our town square. They invited me to watch. I hid in the darkness at the back of the crowd so no one would see me. I heard and saw everything.

"That night Jesus said, *'What good will it be for a man if he gains the whole world but forfeits his soul?'*" (Matthew 16:26).

"I had everything in life, but I was losing my soul. After a year of fighting with my conscience, I went to a Christian. I told him of my struggle. After four more years of conversations with him, I came to Jesus. I asked Him to save my soul and give me peace, and He came to me, but I lost everything."

"What did you lose?" Paul asked.

"Within two months," he sighed, "they took away my wife, my two children, my house and my belongings. They threatened to poison me… everything." His hand cut the air in a sign of finality.

Paul clearly saw the great price he paid, "You also lost your status in that society. You were no longer important to people."

"That is right; everything." he affirmed. "I had to go into hiding until it was safe. People who once were friends wanted to kill me. God led me to a pastor who took me as a son and taught me the Jesus way.

"Even after they stopped trying to kill me, my family continued to lure me to return to my old religion. But I didn't go.

"Then, one day, God brought me a lady who chose to lose everything so she could gain Jesus. We were married and moved to a remote village to live."

To this day no one has heard if Amadou and his wife are still alive, or even if they still follow Jesus.

Many people, like Amadou, leave their family religion and give up everything to follow Jesus. Every day they experience the words of the Apostle Paul, who counted the cost rather than be lost. He wrote, *"I consider everything a loss compared to the surpassing greatness of knowing Christ Jesus my Lord"* (Philippians 3:8).

THOUGHT QUESTIONS:
CHAPTER 28
COUNT THE COST OR BE LOST

Amadou was a very powerful Muslim priest and marabou. Yet, he discovered that everything he could do for himself still would not satisfy his soul. Then, when he followed Jesus, he lost everything, but his loss was not equal to the value of what he gained in following Jesus.

1.   Read Mark 8:34-38—What price does Jesus ask every person to pay in order to be His disciple? Memorize Philippians 3:8.

2.   What did Amadou lose because he chose to follow Jesus? What did he gain?

3.   What must you give up so you can fully follow Jesus?

CHAPTER 29
A LETTER FROM PAUL AND MARIAN

Dear Reader,

Thank you for reading these stories! We pray that you have learned how to better walk with Jesus.

God's highest desire for each of us is that we will glorify Him with our lives. Jesus said, *"Let your light so shine before men that they will see your good works and glorify God in heaven."* (Matthew 6:33). We shine His light with every decision we make and every action we take.

When we decide to follow Him, and go wherever He sends us in this world, He uses us to bring the light of Jesus to others.

May the new thoughts you discovered in these stories encourage you to live your life for Jesus. And if the Holy Spirit sends you to another culture and people, He will not abandon you, but will walk beside you every step of the way.

May the Spirit of Jesus guide you and keep you,

Paul & Marian Keidel

———————

Did you like reading about God-moments?
These are great stories for grandkids, nephews and nieces.
Please give this to a friend or buy more to give away.

Made in United States
North Haven, CT
10 April 2024

51148338R00093